HOW TO START YOUR OWN BUSINESS:
EVEN WITHOUT CAPITAL

GOKE AKINOLA

HOW TO START YOUR OWN BUSINESS: EVEN WITHOUT CAPITAL

Goke Akinola

ISBN: 978-978-957-607-4

Copyright @ 2016

All rights reserved. This book is protected by copyright law of Nigeria. No part of this book should be reprinted without the written permission of the author and publisher.

For more information contact:
Email: gokeget@yahoo.com
Phone: 234 (0) 806 292 9176, 234 (0) 708 142 2110.

Published by:
Geaworth Consult
Plot 9A, Road 3, Ikota Villa Etate,
Lekki, Lagos.

Produced by:
King's Delight Field Ventures
1, Tenibegiloju Street, Iyana-Ipaja, Lagos, Nigeria.
E-mail: kingsdfieldv@gmail.com
Phone: 234 (0) 803 304 1910, 234 (0) 809 841 1965.

DEDICATION

Dedicated to
Elder Felix Eze,
Managing Director/Chief Executive Officer,
F. A. Lovers Nigeria Limited
and Lovers Bakeries Limited,
who inadvertently delivered to me first hand;
the step-by-step details of the business world
and entrepreneurship.

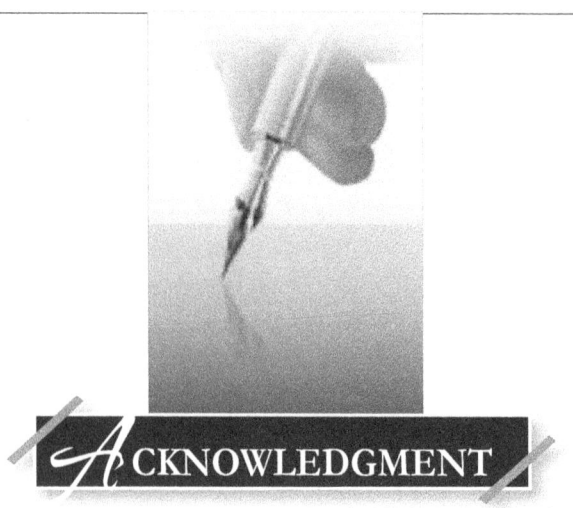

ACKNOWLEDGMENT

A tree does not make a forest. Whatever I am, some people have contributed to my success; I am grateful to them all. To Pastor B.M.G Amosa, on whose table I found the magazine that changed my orientation right from school days. It all started from you. To Deacon Shola Atofarati and his family, my companions in the journey of self-actualization, I acknowledge your friendship and support. To Olowoye Olumide, MD/CEO, Nwannegadi Microfinance Bank Ltd, whose bank financed the first edition of this work, you are a friend indeed. To Rosemary Bakare, who encouraged me all along and assisted in the typing of the manuscript (First Edition), I appreciate you so much.

To Pastor Patrick Romanus and the entire Business Church of The Redeemed Evangelical Mission (TREM), Imo State University, whose invitation to speak on the topic inspired me to put down what time did not permit us to discuss in full, I am very grateful. To Onyebuchi Maduagwu of Skye Bank Plc, Douglas Road, Owerri, who share the same philosophy with me and has been a source of encouragement always. Thank you for being there.

To Mr. Olanrewaju Kashim, MD/CEO, Microcred Nigeria, whose daily encouragement keeps me going, you are a good example. My gratitude goes to Mr. Dayo Afolabi of Dangote Group for always being a source of productive inspiration and sharing vital corporate experiences with me. Many thanks to Adewale Adesola, Kayode Ajayi, Enrico Abutu, Fadilat Baruwa and Israel Omokanye, all of Skye Bank Group, for their roles in the typesetting & proof reading of this work. I am extremely grateful to Pastor Sam. Adeyemi through whom I receive daily inspiration and spiritual guidance. To my wife, Joy and my children, Adeola and Adewale, whose roles make my life journey interesting, you are my world of happiness.

TABLE OF Contents

Page

Dedication — 3
Acknowledgment — 4

Introduction — 8

CHAPTER ONE
Know your business and be free from Poverty — 12

CHAPTER TWO
Developing your Creativity — 32

CHAPTER THREE
Knowledge is Power: Planning is Progress   45

CHAPTER FOUR
Power of Communication and the Place of
Connection   89

CHAPTER FIVE
Power of Opportunity   98

CHAPTER SIX
The Three Laws of Money   106

CHAPTER SEVEN
Consistency and Investment   138

CHAPTER EIGHT
Talents, Choice and Action   145

CHAPTER NINE
Straight to Points: More than 50 Businesses
you can start, even without Capital   156

CHAPTER TEN
Managing the Transition   202

CHAPTER ELEVEN
The Best Way to Start   232

INTRODUCTION

Whatever may be said in praise of poverty, the truth is that poverty still remains the worst disease the human race has ever known. Poverty is instrumental to most other human problems and it is the strength of any epidemic or pandemic. It kills more people than HIV/AIDS. Any nation that takes the fight against poverty for granted is putting its citizens and the upcoming generations in the greatest jeopardy.

Poverty is lack of money to take care of one's needs or legitimate desires. It is the lack of power or resources to achieve legitimate and worthy goals. Riches is the opposite of poverty, it is the ability to meet your financial needs as and

INTRODUCTION

when due. Riches is possessing enough that makes you live the type of life you desire. It enables you to **'live your life in your own way'**. It empowers you to take control of your life financially. You cannot know a man's true character until he has enough money to do all he seriously wished.

Even a man without money does not know his own character. Money helps to reveal the innermost intention of a man. It helps to demonstrate your innermost values. Riches have to do with freedom from financial embarrassment. It is the ability to meet your needs and those of your family with positive legacy for generations after you.

One thing is sure; you cannot be working for somebody and be thinking of getting rich. It does not happen that way. The best employment can only succeed in making you an average man. Good job may help you live a decent life but it will never put you in charge of your situation. It will never put you in control of your life. And no matter how decent he looks, a servant is still a servant, period. Call him **"civil servant", "public servant"** or any other name, a servant does not serve himself. His livelihood is at someone's mercy.

This book will not condemn working for somebody, but it condemns the attitude of planning your life on an employment or a job. It helps you to understand the basics of the business life. It teaches the laws of money. With this book in your hand, you have no right to be jobless or unemployed. No one, after reading this book, is permitted to be jobless or remain a

INTRODUCTION

full time job seeker. Students reading this book in their undergraduate years are in for basic adventure of the things that will equip their minds on financial freedom, even from school. For them, looking for a paid job is going to be a matter of choice.

If you are employed at present, you face three alternatives, sooner or later. You will either be retired, be retrenched or you resign. But it is more honorable to resign. This book will help you to plan your exit from the first day on the job. Never wait until you will be retired because by then you may no longer have enough strength to face the challenges of getting other things done. Most retirees don't do anything sustainable with their gratuities or retirement benefit. Why? Because it takes time to learn the basics of the business world.

During your learning period, you will be at the mercies of those people that have been there all the years. You realize that you are only serving the learned during that period of learning. It is a normal thing for you to fall prey to the learned, because in a way you must pay them goodwill for all their years of experience in the business. But the worst aspect of it is that most retirees would finish their gratuities during that period of learning, without making a single profit. What of the fact that you are not even sure of the gratuity, your employer may decide not to pay and there is little you can do about it, at least in Nigeria of today? Thank God for the contributory pension scheme. However, the pension money is not to make you rich,

INTRODUCTION

it is only to keep body and soul together. So, the best time to learn is now.

"It is good for a man that he bears the yoke in his youth" says the Holy Bible, Lamentations 3:27. If you want to do something, the time is now. Never plan your life on pension! Now that you are collecting salary, it is hard to keep body and soul together, how much more when you are collecting pension. The time to learn is now; the time to act is now. Life is what you make out of it. It is all a matter of choice.

Finally, I say unto you; "To be poor is natural; to remain poor is a choice". "To fail is natural; to remain a failure is foolishness". This book empowers you to make the decision to be free financially. The choice is yours.

KNOW YOUR BUSINESS AND BE FREE FROM POVERTY

1

WHATEVER may be said in praise of poverty, the truth is that it is not possible to live a complete and successful life except one is rich. No one can attain the fullness of his potentials in an organized society unless he has money to do so.

In an organized society, the things you need for the full development of body and soul must be bought. And you need money to do that. "No money, no deal". Man's right to life means his right to have the free and unrestricted use of all things which may be necessary to his fullest mental, spiritual and physical development. To do this, he must be rich; have enough money to purchase those things. Riches here does not mean to be contented with little, to be contented with little is only a figurative definition of riches. No man ought to be satisfied with little if he is capable of using and enjoying more. The man who owns all he wants for living is rich and this is the desire of all men. Believe it or not, everybody wants to be rich. That desire is natural. There is nothing wrong in wanting to get rich. The man who does not desire to have money enough to buy all he wants is abnormal.

The question is, are all men rich? The answer is obvious, it is absolutely 'No'. The next is, can all be rich, have enough money for living? Yes. But why are all men not rich? Because many people get many things wrong, many do not have the needed knowledge for money making. Many do not have the true knowledge, the knowledge of God, knowledge of themselves and the knowledge of the world in which we live and its system.

The greatest objective of any human system is human development. And the central objective of development is for man to master himself and his environment. Wrong or inadequate knowledge of self and the world we live in is the root of poverty all through the ages. While it could be reasonably argued that it is the knowledge of God that is the most critical, the true knowledge of God will ultimately lead to the discovery of yourself and the world around you.

I must also add that the concepts of business, productivity and wealth creation revolve around man and his environment, that is, meeting the personal and societal needs of people and physical needs of the environment. Any man who wants to be rich on sustainable basis must first align his thought with this concept. He must fully and passionately be committed to meeting human and environmental needs. He must learn to add value to man and his environment. That is the undisputable way to riches, joy and happiness. Do this consistently and money will come looking for you.

One major thing that the most men and women of our generation are getting wrong is the concept of riches. They do not know what it takes to be rich, have success and fulfillment in life. One thing you must know is that to get rich and become fulfilled in life, you must invest your life on doing something, something profitable. The thing you invest your life on must be profitable and rewarding enough to provide what you need for a comfortable life, at least in the long run. The only thing that can give you this end is your own business. Paid employment cannot do that for you, because in paid job, you undertake to do another man's business for him. Be sure, your employer did not establish his business for you. He did for himself, to make him rich and comfortable.

Everything that happens in that business is to satisfy the owner's end. It is called maximizing the owners' or shareholders' wealth. And this is not bad. If you want something for your own satisfaction, you should go and establish your own business. You cannot be rich working for somebody. Of course, working for someone can provide you the platform to learn and legitimately establish a model for lunching out on your own.

No employer pays you in order for you to become rich or wealthy. Decision to be rich must of a necessity be a personal decision. Why does your employer pay you? He does for you to stay alive and have enough strength to build his business for him. In the corporate world, we may give many other laudable reasons why we pay our employee the wages we pay them. However, the real reason in the core of our reasoning is for the employee to have enough strength to continue to work for us.

Even when you are still in somebody's employment, you must be sure that the employment is helping you and leading you to building your own someday. At every stage of your life, especially during your adulthood, you must consciously invest your resources-money, time and energy in identifying, starting, building and developing your own business. That is the only way to abundance, as far as money is concerned.

Throughout this book, we will look at four things via various dimensions, using different mind blowing approaches:

First, we will define and explain the concept business or your own business.
Second, we will look at the primary things you must know in order to start and grow your own business. We look at those things available to you which are more important than startup capital or money.

Third, we will look at different types of business you can engage yourself in, even when you have no start-up capital.

Fourth, we will discuss how you can start your own business.

All these will be discussed passionately using different analysis and explanations through the eleven chapters of this book.

YOUR OWN BUSINESS
I need to take a look at some other terms that confuse with the term "business". This is because it is the ability to properly distinguish between these terms and the term "your own business", that will make you to consciously make efforts to start and grow your own business. Another essence of definitions and explanations here is to provoke critical thinking which is necessary for developing productivity mentality in you.

JOB
Contemporary English dictionary defines a job as "regular paid employment, a piece of work, something hard to do." Surely, it does not talk of satisfaction or fulfillment. It talks about paid employment, but no mention as to whether your pay justifies your effort or not. From the definition, there is no emphasis on your gifting, talent or natural interest. Of course, there are thousands of people who daily engage in things that have no bearing with their interest, gift or talent. They keep up

with various activities, just to keep body and soul together. These are the job mentality people, who see life as a survival race.

The definition also talks of something hard to do. To do another man's business is always very hard. That is why it has been proven that no man can use more than 15% of his natural ability or potential working for somebody. Because, most of the time you are not happy with the work or the schedule, but you just have to do it. Napoleon Hill in his "Law of Success" described "the grievous bondage of having to come to a fixed place, for a fixed number of hours, within a fixed period of the day for everyday of a life time".

The school system, especially in Nigeria, prepares people for job and job market only, not for life's satisfaction or fulfillment. I conducted a survey some years back and I discovered that of all the houses in the area where we live, people who are not educated own about 70%. By people who are not educated I mean those without the formal university or higher education. Observation around that same place has shown that more than 50% of private businesses are owned by people who are without formal education. Where are the University and Polytechnic graduates? They are busy looking for paid jobs, jobs created by people who did not go to school. What an irony? Even if you have to work for somebody, it should not be a lifetime affair, use the time to get the necessary knowledge, connection and money for your own business.

That should not in any way hinder you from giving your employer his just and fair due, in line with the employment contract.

Ask yourself this question and through a careful observation provide answer to it. How many graduates of business administration do you think Nigerian universities and polytechnics turn out each year? Of all the successful small, medium and big businesses around you, how many of them are owned or managed by those graduates of business administration? As an extension of this question, let us introduce another important question. In our universities and polytechnics, we got the privilege of being taught by experienced Academic Doctors and Professors? Let us narrow the analysis to the field of business management and administration. How many of these our Doctors and Professors have either managed a business before or can even manage one successfully?

The reason for this analysis is to make you know that, if you are thinking of achieving financial freedom some day, you may need to jettison some of the scholastic ideas injected into you from the formal school system. If your definition of business is the one handed down to you by the academic scholars, you may find it difficult to understand the important ideas that lead to financial freedom, which are the main goals of this book. Do all the above suggest that formal education is evil or unnecessary? The answer is absolute 'No'. You only need to know both the importance and the limitation of formal education. This will enable you to put it to the right use, if you have got it. If you have not got formal education, you will need to learn how to overcome the limitations of lack of formal education.

The trend is not limited to our school system. Our entire formal sector does not support or promote independence and innovation. This is understandable since the formal school system is the one that produce human resources for the formal sector– public and private. Many key players in the public sector today advise youths not to look for paid jobs. They are quick to advise youths to look for things they can do on their own. Ironically, many of these public players who have reached retirement age would rather swear false affidavit to reduce their age and continue in public service. The truth is that they are also afraid of trying any other thing outside salary job.

I look at the life styles and dispositions of many of my colleagues in the banking industry and I feel extremely sorry. Many, who are in charge of billions of naira of depositors' money are individuals who cannot properly manage a million naira of their own. They can process a billion naira loan for other people but they cannot manage a million naira shop of their own. The truth is that very many people we have in the banking industry today are those who are completely useless without the banking job. And how many of us are going to be on that job for a life time? The most unsecured job in Nigeria since the economic meltdown in 2008/2009 is a banking job.

The crash in the capital market affected people from every sector of our economy; including the poor and the middle class who were lured to buy shares with their life savings. But in my own analysis bankers were among the biggest victims of the market crash. There are many who did not have any savings despite the fat salaries after consolidation. Even though majority lived expensive lives, there are still some with little savings. These classes of people invested their little savings in the capital market and borrow more sums for speculating in shares. Those without savings also borrowed huge sums to speculate in the capital market. The major reason is that many of these people did not know any other form of investment. And since you can wholly leave your shares in the hands of company managers and stock brokers, they all went for that cheap alternative.

I was told of a man that left bank job with very huge severance package out of which he built a house in the capital city of his state of origin. Since he knew no other thing he could do, he invested the remaining money in the stock market. He also went ahead to obtain further huge sums of money in bank loan, using his new house as collateral security. Everything he put in the market. Shortly after these big stock market investments, the market crashed. The natural outcome was that the bank foreclosed on the house. He lost the money, he lost the house. He suddenly developed hypertension and died.

OCCUPATION

It is normal in any personal data form to see a place asking you to fill in your occupation. But no one ever asks for your business. Our society frowns at an adult without an occupation. Nobody however sees anything wrong in somebody without a business called his own or any definite plan to get one. To me, that is a misplaced priority by our society. The position will be clearer after we might have defined business in this context. You will know that occupation is not necessarily synonymous with business. Just like a job and business are not necessarily the same in meaning.

Your occupation is whatever gets you occupied, anyhow it may be. And our society and system says you must be occupied with something, whether you are adequately rewarded or not, whether it gives you the promise of a better tomorrow or not. The system does not also place any emphasis on what value you add or how productively you are occupied. The emphasis is on efforts not on results. Until this mentality is changed, we will not be able to build a developed and value oriented system. Value orientation is the hallmark of a developed society. Efforts are very important because, we cannot create value without appropriate efforts been applied. However, any effort that does not result to value in the long run is useless. It is only efforts properly directed that bring results.

The priority of the society must have been partly reinforced by the belief that an idle hand is the devil's workshop. The truth is that an idle hand is primarily a product of an idle mind. An idle hand, is the devil's workshop. The real devil's empire is an idle mind. People's hands must not only be occupied, but their minds must also be productively engaged. Further analysis will confirm to us that being occupied does not automatically mean being productive. Of course, thousands of people have learnt to be busy doing nothing. English dictionary defines occupation as "a way of spending time". You need more than an occupation; you need a business called your own. That will engage your hands and your entire being. It is only at this point a man can experience fulfillment.

EMPLOYMENT

To employ somebody means to use him or his service to perform work in return for pay. The employee does not decide or design the work; he is only being used to perform it. No employer can make you comfortable in life as you ought to be, because he did not establish his business to make you comfortable. He established it for himself. Even when he pretends to love you, he does not actually love you; he only likes your services to grow his own business. Some big corporations that try to offer a lot to retain their employee only do so to prevent the employee from thinking of his own business and for him to continue to serve the employer's purpose.

It is a matter of time, you will either resign or retire or be retrenched. The point must be clear here. Being in an employment does not mean being productive. It does not mean being fulfilled in life. You can even be in an employment and be paid large, fat salaries without personal fulfillment. There is a level of fulfillment that can only come doing what you can do most with passion.

I must admit that it is still possible to find your life's business in another person's employment. This happens to a few people in life. However, the fact that it happens only to a few makes it an exception. Even the exceptional people know that life does not run on exceptions; it runs on principles. All the major advancements, discoveries, inventions and developments throughout the ages have been based on verifiable principles that can be generalized and work for anyone.

The purpose of this book is to teach principles rather than exceptions. You don't need to be a genius for a principle to work for you. All you need is to follow the rules and the result will be automatic.

Development of our world has never been a product of success that is reserved for a class of people. True development in human history has always been a product of applying principles that are generally available and applicable to everyone. Every developing country can become developed if only it applies enough courage and commitment to do what the developed countries do. With time, a poor man will become rich if only he has enough courage and commitment to think and do things the way the rich do.

CAREER

"A career is a job or profession for which one is trained and which one intends to follow for part or the whole of one's life time". Do you see anything like money, comfort, satisfaction or pleasure in the definition of career? Your career does not automatically give you those essentials except you have developed your own business using the instrumentality of your career. Thousands of people today are trying to build careers around areas different from their areas of dominant interests and passion.

What we are doing here is to teach how life can be enjoyable and rewarding by doing what you enjoy. It is about determining the type of life you want to live. This you can achieve and enjoy without being held down by the "lack of capital" syndrome. The emphasis will rather be on creativity, productivity, interest, passion, trust and so on. All these are called '**social capital**' in the business world. They are more important than physical capital. For you to see what these truly are, you need a change of mentality. This, I believe this book will make possible for you. If you are not ready for a change of mentality and orientation, you may not need to read further.

PROFESSION

A profession is "a form of employment, especially one that is possible only for an educated person and after training (such as law, medicine, or teaching)". Here again the emphasis is on formal education or academic training not on money or

fulfillment or satisfaction. You are a professional in a field if you know enough in that field that you can be regarded as an authority. You are a professor if you have acquired and demonstrated enough knowledge in your field to the satisfaction of the institution that made you a professor.

But being a professor or a professional does not automatically give you the money you need in life. It is only doing your own business, the right business in the right way that gives you financial freedom and independence. That is why professors have to go on industrial strike before their employers can listen to them, increase their pay or improve their condition of service. When you are in your own business you don't go on strike in order to get more money. When you need more money you reorganize your business and re-strategize.

Your business is in the place where your interest and passion lie. Your success is in the place of your interest and passion. In our study of executive compensation management, it was a general consensus that organizations pay for marginal productivity of an employee rather than the employee's qualifications or certificates. Your certificates are your properties. What matters to any organization is the value you can add to their business.

This is not to undermine the place of special knowledge or professionalism in any endeavor. But the truth is that somebody must be able to make business sense out of the special knowledge in order for the knowledge to benefit you and the society. You must also know that there are businesses that do not require specialized knowledge in order to make you comfortable.

To think that the level of wealth built by Henry Ford is a product of his technical knowledge of automobile engineering is an absurdity. To assume that Andrew Carnegie's wealth is a product of his technical knowledge of the steel industry is highly unthinkable. Where special knowledge is required, such knowledge could be purchased. It does not also require huge money called capital for anyone to start business. What is required is what this book is set to teach you.

BUSINESS
To start with, let me summarize what I have said so far.
- The terms job, employment, occupation, career and profession are not synonymous to business.
- They are not prerequisites for being in business. None of them is a must have for a successful business life.
- They are not contrary to business. An employed person can go into business, a career person can grow his own business, so also a professor and even a student.

All of the above can and are always very useful in business.
It must be noted that when any of these stands alone without being applied to business, it can only succeed in making you an average person.

It follows therefore that if you are a student, you should look beyond hoping for a job or employment after school. Get yourself ready for a successful life. Even if you have to take employment, it must be a matter of choice, and you choose the one that will help you build your own business or secure your financial future.

If you are a policy maker, now or in future, ensure a school systems that will teach people how to make money for living, as an essential course.

Finally, I define your business as **'the process of you engaging what you have to create the world of your choice for yourself and adding value to the society'**.

WHAT IS "YOUR OWN BUSINESS"?

Robert Kiyosaki, the American author of "**Rich Dad Poor Dad**" said business is the one that can make your money work for you.

I define business as that which you engages your resources in for adequate reward. You reap as you sow, no cheating. Your business makes use of what you have or what you can have. It does not ask for what you don't have before satisfying you. You control your business; your business does not control you. Remember, the employer controls the employee. Ultimately, it leads to financial freedom. Normally, your business should outlive you.

What then is your own business? It is the one that you enjoy and is fun rather than work. In my own case, getting knowledge, impacting knowledge is just natural to me. And that is my business. It is one thing I will protect jealously in my life, that is my first consideration as to whether I should take a job or not. Anything I will do, anywhere I will go that will hinder me from updating my existing knowledge, gathering current information and using it to motivate and encourage others, I will not do such no matter how much money you promise me. There may be things that give money but do not give joy and fulfillment and satisfaction. Even when I had to take up a paid job, I did primarily to prepare a platform for my own business. As much as godliness demands that I should do my duties on the job with all diligence and satisfy my employer, I must not also forget my own goal for living, my business. I use opportunities provided to me daily for that end.

You too have many untapped talents that you can use to start and grow your own business, on full time or part time basis. Start by making a list of your hobbies and interests. The first job I took after my Youth Service was the one that paid little money and without a promise of something fantastic in the nearest future. In fact, my monthly salary was less than the total of my local and federal allowances during the NYSC service year. My focus then was not the money but how the job will help me to start from somewhere and equip myself for business life, a life of satisfaction and fulfillment. How it was going to lead me to financial liberty was very important to me.

Of course, what I am doing today might not have been possible if I had started with a banking job. To a business minded person, money is not the first factor. If you grow your own business your business will give you all the money you need and give you freedom with it. Less I forget to mention this: you cannot be rich working for somebody. You may have so much money to spend as an employee. The day you lose that job, you will discover you have been a poor person all the while.

WISDOM OF SOLOMON
Much as I do not intend making this book a religious information manual, I still find an example from the Bible that can help you understand the principle I am teaching. It is from a statement by the wisest man that ever lived, King Solomon the son of David, the third King of Israel.

Why was Solomon referred to as the wisest? The first reason is, because God called him the wisest. So, God gave him the wisdom and the title to it. Another reason was because Solomon's wisdom was very practical. It was wisdom that produced results, wisdom that solved his problems and those of his nation, his generation and generations after him. His wisdom, indeed, outlived him.

The wisdom of Solomon gave him peace and plenty. He never lacked anything good. His enemies were permanently under his control. You need to learn from such a man. Of course, human wisdom is relative. And so, God compared Solomon's wisdom with the opportunities available to him and challenges he had to face. And God concluded that his wisdom was greater than those of his generation, those before him and those after him.

KNOW YOUR BUSINESS AND BE FREE FROM POVERTY

WHAT THEN DID SOLOMON SAY?
"Seest thou a man diligent in his business? He shall stand before Kings; he shall not stand before mean men" Proverbs 22:29.

Diligence in his business, not in another man's business. It is investing your talents and gifts in your business that leads to greatness. When you are in another person's employment, it is that person you are building and not yourself. The contract of employment is that you should build the employer. Even though it also implies that your employer should build you, but most employer never do that, and there is little you can do about it, especially in an economy full of joblessness. Even in employment, there is a level of growth you cannot attain until you have learnt to see the work as your own. It is only at that level that you can generate a significant passion to succeed on the job.

More importantly, complete diligence is not possible in another man's business. No matter how faithful and committed you are in another person's business, you will still discover that you will do better if it were your own business. Experts have confirmed that an average person cannot use more than 15% of his potentials working for another person. It is a natural thing. When you are working for somebody, there are times you have good ideas that can greatly transform the business. But, it is either you are not privileged to express your idea or the owner or the authorities of the business do not accept your idea. What then will you do? Keep quiet and allow your good idea to die inside you? Don't die doing other person's business.

THE INSIGHT OF JACOB

There is another vital lesson you can learn from the Bible on this subject. It is from Jacob the son of Isaac, the grandson of Abraham and the brother of Esau. You remember now?

His case was similar to that of an average employee. He was an employee of Laban, his father-in-law. He worked for years with no definite plan for his future. No plan for his financial and material freedom. His wages or condition of services was changed ten times at the discretion of Laban and to Laban's advantage. At a time he became wise. He discovered that nobody would plan his freedom for him. He then said; **"when shall I provide for mine own house also"**. Genesis 30:30b. That is, when I shall plan for my own freedom, for my own business, and my own future.

My advice to every employee is to plan for his resignation or retirement from the first day on the job. It is not always easy, but it is worth it and it pays. It will also help you to be a good man on the job, because, you will need to develop yourself, and that will reflect on the job you are doing. Personal development and career development will always go together.

The warning here is that you should not become dishonest because you want to start your own at all cost. Instead, you plan and work hard. Most times, people become dishonest because of lack of plan and self-development. They become so desperate when they suddenly discovered time is almost out or where the income could no longer take care of their basic needs. Avoid crash program, set your priority right from the onset.

DEVELOPING YOUR CREATIVITY

2

Individuals and business organizations that are known for creativity practice a number of simple strategies. It is that practice of these strategies that makes them remain creatively alive and active. Anybody can learn the strategies, practice them and they will work for him. Remember, we are all born with creative abilities. It follows, therefore, that a successful organization is made up of creative minds. All you need is put the creative man on the inside of you to work. I will point out some of the strategies; they are useful for individuals as well as for organizations.

In business, your creativity is more important than capital. That is why successful organizations look for creative people. They are ready to pay them for their creativity. It takes a creative mind to get the capital and to be able to manage it. There are people who have money and are looking for creative people into whose hands they can commit their money. Many people who complain of lack of capital to do business are actually suffering from lack of creativity. Creativity is not just a natural gift or talent, it is what you can cultivate and develop. There are strategies for developing your creativity. I will point out some of the strategies in the following lines:

Make a Commitment to Creativity
When you are in business, your future success depends on your ability to come up with new products, new services, and new ways to get things done. Companies do establish department of Research and Development as a commitment to creativity and continuity of the business.

One way that large, innovative companies commit themselves to innovation is by requiring that a minimum percentage of sales or revenue come from relatively new products and services.

This is a simple concept that an individual starting or growing a personal business can use. Set a goal to derive a minimum percentage of your income per year or per month from new activities and new ideas. Commit a stated percentage of your current income to acquiring new knowledge for financial freedom.

My Personal Example
I remember, as a graduate, I made up my mind not to carry the same certificate for upwards of three years. That makes me

more committed to getting additional knowledge. Another commitment I made was that I would not earn the same income for more than six months. That particularly has set me on the part of new ideas on how to make more money. If my income remains the same for close to six months, I begin to think, meditate, seek information and ask questions on how to make more money. This will certainly leave me with a lot of alternatives for critical consideration. Should I change my job or ask my employer for more pay? Should I look for additional way, to generate income on part time basis? Should I increase my investment from my current income and so on?

These commitments have set me on the part of creativity and progress for the past fifteen years, at least. It has delivered me from waste of time and energy, because at every particular time, there is something very important I have to do. No time to waste. If you are already in business, you can make that commitment that your business will not remain the same for one year without new ideas or innovations or products. It will help you to get committed to creativity and innovation. Striving to meet an innovative goal will keep your business from getting stale as years go by. "**Necessity is the mother of inventions**".

Since I started earning money, there is a significant percentage of my income that goes into acquisition of knowledge every year. I have invested on books over the years. In my library you will find motivational books, business books, professional books, and medical books, spiritual or religious books.

DEVELOPING YOUR CREATIVITY

Before I started reading law in the university, I had law related books like the 1979 Constitution of Nigeria, the 1999 Constitution of Nigeria and even the 2011 amendment in my library. I had books on laws of contract, hire purchase, partnership, personal and company income tax laws, Companies and Allied Matters Act (CAMA), Banks and Other Financial Institutions Act (BOFIA). I have books on first aid, health sciences and personal fitness. All these have a way of reflecting on your life and business performance. Whether I read all of them and how I read them are questions for another day.

Knowledge has a way of increasing your confidence. This is particularly so when your knowledge has a general application to life or specific application to your area of endeavor. Increased confidence naturally produces high level of energy in the confident man. And high level of energy and enthusiasm go together. All these will lead to high level of productivity and performance.

I worked as an accountant and a financial controller in a particular private company. It was 5-five years all together. My performance was excellent to my employer - the company's chairman and his consultants. Some of my co-workers did not like my gut. However, they could never fault my performance and commitment and loyalty to the company.

During the period I did a number of things to generate additional income for myself. At a time, I was distributing GSM recharge vouchers. At another time, I was printing the voucher myself while I had a lot of retailers I distribute to. At one time I was selling new and fairly used GSM phones. There was a time I was into distributorship of a particular brand of toilet soap. Then I was doing management consultancy services to many small and medium businesses within that region. I had private consultancy office with employees working for me. Most times I return to that private office as I close daily from the regular employment. During that time, I was doing my professional examinations and after passing the final stage, I became a lecturer at the professional training centre.

The fact is that, I had no reason to hide the fact that I do any of these things from my employer. Even though my employment with him was supposed to be a full time employment, my chairman never objected my doing additional activities for additional income. Of course, I never left anything undone which I was supposed to do. I rather did more than expected of me on the job. I rather gave some business advice that was not within my core responsibilities. Those pieces of advice all worked very well. This was simply because I read wide. The chairman even patronized my other businesses. I supplied recharge cards to him and his family members. When I was doing internet connection for other businesses and private homes on consultancy basis, I did install internet facility for the office and the chairman's house. I was paid accordingly.

I knew sometimes he got uncomfortable with my being too aggressive, particularly as he feels I might leave the company at any time soon. Yet, I was about the closest staff to him and other staff including my seniors felt the chairman listens to my advice always. We had to disagree on principles at different times, yet we would resolve the differences and get on with the business. I tendered my resignation three different times when the chairman had to call me to renegotiate conditions of service rather than allow me leave the company. It was at my fourth resignation he agreed to let me go reluctantly when I made it clear I was not ready for renegotiation. My resignation was accepted this time, not without my promising that if he needs my services at anytime I will be available either on volunteer or consultancy basis.

Knowledge will always make your face to shine.

Emphasize your Core Competence
Find your core competences and use them to create something unique. Focus on business or industry that builds your strengths. Your strengths are your core competences. Your best chance for creative success will come from building on those things you know about and have experience in.

I remember my encounter with a successful businessman I respected so much. I asked him why he chose to go into his particular business, which he has now built to greatness over the years. The man simply told me, "**because that is what I know how to do**". The obvious lesson to learn here is "**know your**self". Somebody said, "**He who knows himself is wise**". Trying to get creative or innovative in an area you know little or nothing about is usually money – losing and wasteful proposition.

For instance, my core competence is in creating and

DEVELOPING YOUR CREATIVITY

communicating information that helps people achieve their life's goals, especially in the area of business, self employment, self reliance and maximum achievement. Hence, any products or services I develop revolve around that.

Just that I discovered very early after my graduation, that my mind works faster than my hand. I am an idea merchant. I think it, describe it adequately and sell it to others. And the ideas always work. Because I put quality thoughts into it and I can do more by concentrating on thinking out solution in a problem situation. That may surprise you, but that is what I have discovered and analyzed carefully. I can direct in such a way that very difficult tasks become very simple. I can co-ordinate people to greater achievement. I see possibilities where a lot of people see impossibility. It has always worked for me. I function better with ideas than with detailed technicalities.

In the recent times, I have seen people I advised and who took my advice achieving success exponentially. It always works for them. And so, I try to develop myself so people can get information for success from me always. This is something I enjoy doing even without any monetary compensation.

That is the way all developed societies were built. A few more serious people concentrate on thinking out solution, while a large number of others execute. The solution crafting process may be called research and development or any other name. The point is that the more successful institutions are those that learn to separate strategy from operations. Strategists are few. This is because only one strategist can provide jobs for

DEVELOPING YOUR CREATIVITY

thousands or millions of operators. Operators work with their hands while strategists work with their minds. Both classes are very important but one normally makes more impacts than the other.

Look for Creative Partners
You are not likely going to find new ideas by locking yourself in your room or office, thinking. Sometimes it works like that but it is not always and it costs more that way. Ideas come by interacting with people. You need to observe and identify their problems, think of possible solutions to those problems. You get to know more by asking.

The type of people you surround yourself with also matters. Don't surround yourself with people who, everything about them is problem and failure. You avoid people who only have problem mentality and not solution mentality. That people have problems is not strange, that they don't believe in or hope for solution is the irony.

You need to think along with the problem solvers. Listen to people who have and are still getting problems solved, men of possibility. Like that, you will develop your creative and innovative ability and remain creative and innovative.

You must create opportunities for both interaction and solitude. The more you interact and learn from others, the more ideas you will generate. Make it your practice to meet regularly with others. Customers, friends, families and other entrepreneurs can provide you with the information stimulation, and feedback you need to create new solutions you need to solve your problems or refine any new ideas you have. The key is to choose those who are positive, creative and supportive.

However, interaction alone is not enough. You need enough solitude to be able to digest all you have got through interaction. You will find time to diffuse the information into your system and then reproduce it in your own form. And you will need time apart to do that. Solitude is very important for analytical and critical thinking and meditation. You must of necessity create time for that too.

Give yourself the right to be wrong
When an idea does not work, consider it as part of the price you pay for future success and learn from it. If you keep trying and learning, you will eventually hit a big money making idea that will compensate many times over for all the money – losers.

When you are in new business, it is natural for you to lose some money at the beginning. Usually, you lose money to people who have been in that business for long. They know the terrain very well. And so, they can manipulate. You can lose money to the manipulation by some of the bad elements who are more experienced than you are.

The fear of losing money at this early stage is the reason why many cannot venture into their own businesses. You reduce your losses by studying a particular trade or business well before investing in it. However, no matter how much you study, you cannot know enough to match people with hand-on experience in the field.

Any money you lose, see it as the cost you have to pay for your ignorance. By the time you have gained the necessary knowledge and experience, you will get the money back hundred times over.

Relax and have fun with your ideas
Although, you need to keep focused on your ideas and don't allow them to slip away. One way you can do that is to ensure you write them down as they come to you. However, rigid, structured, serious thinking and behavior is one sure way to kill creativity.

Creativity flourishes best in an environment where there is a relaxing spirit of playfulness. Relaxing as you are thinking will stimulate creativity. So, don't make the mistake of trying to be serious and have no time to relax. There is time to be serious and time to relax, they are equally important. Let your mind wonder. Avoid being too careful. That way, you will be able to come up with some profitable ideas.

Believe in your creative power
Finally, believe in your creative power and you will get the ideas you want. Believe you are creative and your subconscious will create the reality. Each of us has different level of creativity. We all manifest certain level of creativity when it becomes very necessary. If you came face to face with a lion, you will manifest a level of creativity that you never believed you possess. At least you will take enough steps to make you escape.

Necessity, they say is the mother of inventions. You can intentionally make that necessity your daily reality. If necessity becomes a reality, creativity will certainly become a reality. Intentionally put yourself in position where you must come up with some sort of solution or alternatives.

CREATIVITY QUESTIONNAIRE
When you are trying to do better things or do things better, it is pertinent you form the habit of asking relevant questions. Those questions that you answered will provide solutions to existing problems. They will also bring to limelight the existing problems that have been overlooked or abandoned.

Take a product, service or anything you are trying to improve upon and ask a series of questions about it. Examples of such questions are given below:
- Is there a new way to do it?
- Can you make it bigger or smaller?
- Can you add something to it, subtract something from it, or rearrange the order of it?
- Can you combine this with something?
- What if you do the opposite of this?
- Can something be substituted for it? How can you make it better, faster or cheaper?
- What else can be adapted?
- How can you give this a new twist?
- What if you don't do anything?
- How can you make this more sellable?

DEVELOPING YOUR CREATIVITY

Asking the right questions often cause your imagination to come up with new and good ideas. Make sure these questions are written down. They must not be abandoned. You must find answers to them, also in writing.

After you have written down all the questions, the best thing is to then take the questions one per time to think through. An answer to a question will usually bring up another question. You should never be discouraged, because the more you sincerely and realistically think through the closer you are to a useful solution to a human problem.

I must mention this. Even when you failed to generate a valid idea or solution from this exercise at any particular time, you have not lost anything. As a beginner, you may think you have wasted all the time and energy invested on the exercise. I can tell you this; if you have done the exercise with the commitment it deserves, you have come out a better person. You must have learnt lots of vital lessons along the line.

Your mind and your thinking process can never remain the same. Those lessons are equally very important because they get you closer to the place you are going. They get you closer to real creativity. Your ability to think through must have improved.

You remember the story of Thomas Edison? Edison is one of the greatest inventors the world has ever produced. After he carried out experiments more than a thousand times without a result, he refused to agree with the people's opinion that he has failed a thousand times. He said he has only learnt one thousand ways not to do it.

That is the key; the mindset. This is a major difference between failures and achievers.

KNOWLEDGE IS POWER: PLANNING IS PROGRESS

3

POWER OF KNOWLEDGE
"Knowledge is power". Nobody can be truly successful in life without the right and adequate knowledge. You need knowledge for living; you also need knowledge for business.

Most people are poor today because they don't have value for knowledge. If you don't have value for knowledge you will die of ignorance.

The most deadly decease in our generation is not HIV/AIDS. It is not tuberculoses or malaria. Hypertension and diabetics are deadly, but they are not the biggest problems of this generation. Ignorance is the problem. And poverty is usually the direct result of ignorance. Have you observed that the more value a nation attached to knowledge, the more successful or developed that nation will be? Where there is adequate knowledge, the effect of the so called deadly and terminal deceases will be minimized.

An average American should be prone to diabetics and hypertension more than a Nigerian. This is essentially because of the type of food they are exposed to and their feeding habits. Many Americans eat processed junk food. They eat fat and have to deal with obesity as a routine. But life expectancy in America is far higher than that of Nigeria. And it has always been higher. Life expectance refers to "**how long an average person in a society is expected to live, under normal circumstances**". At the time when life expectancy in the US was 82years, it was 52years in Nigeria. 30 years is a very wide gap. There are reliable reports that confirm there are actually more cases of obesity, diabetics and hypertension reported in America. However, knowledge has enabled the US and her citizens to put these deadly deceases under control.

What is the difference? Knowledge is the difference. Information is the difference. Direct result of ignorance is poverty. And nothing endangers human lives in this generation like poverty. Most problems confronting our society today are direct results of poverty. Unfortunately, we are in a society full of pretence. We pretend often that poverty is not the problem, hunger is not the problem and ignorance is not the problem. The poor man wants to do everything to cover up his poverty and appear outside like a rich man. The very ignorant want to pretend to know everything. Our society needs a change, radical change. The change must start from the mindsets of individuals.

KNOWLEDGE THAT DELIVERS RESULTS

When we solve the problem of ignorance, we would have largely addressed the problem of poverty. Ignorance is the number one cause of poverty. When I talk about knowledge, I mean the right knowledge. It is only the right knowledge that produces results. You have to know that Africa has not always been in ignorance compared to the other parts of the world. Our forefathers knew a lot that they could even turn day to night. The question is whether that knowledge has produced results in progress and development? Even for your business success, you need to first identify the type of knowledge that is useful for you, then you go for it.

My greatest concern for Nigerians of our generation is that we lose value for knowledge every day. We all look for money instead of knowledge. In the history of man, money has never improved the world. It is knowledge that improves the world. Knowledge gives us mastery of the world we live in and improves the quality of life we live. Money or riches have always been by-products. There are some things you will know and apply or practice that money has no choice than to come to you.

I am not talking of only business knowledge. I am talking of all round knowledge; knowledge for living. Business knowledge is just one of them, even though a very important one. The essence of this book is to show you that money is just a tool.

Knowledge tells you how to get the tools and how to use it. Of course you should know that the 'real' problem of many of us is not money. It is the right use of money. Money is always there.

And money has come or will come to each of us at different times. Knowledge will help you to engage money and put it to productive use. When you see small money and you use it properly, it will stay with you. It will also attract its likes. Then, money will multiply in your hands. That is the only proven way to lasting riches and wealth.

LABOUR TURNOVER VS MONEY TURNOVER
Labour turnover refers to "**the ratio of the number of employees that leave a company through attrition, dismissal, or resignation during a period to the number of employee on payroll during the same period**". "**It refers to the number or percentage of workers who leave an organization and are replaced by new employees**".

My objective here is not to engage you through a discussion on labour turnover. I am not also out on an argument as to whether labour turnover is a certain indication that an organization is good or bad. Certainly labour turnover is a key factor in analyzing the performance of an organization, a management team or a management style. But the truth is that there are desirable turnovers and undesirable turnovers.

A single book will not be enough for a thorough discussion on employees' turnover. However, our objective here is to draw a learning analogy between labour turnover and "**money turnover**". By money turnover we mean how money comes to and leaves an individual or even an organization or a society. We have mentioned earlier that money comes to everyone at different times, at different rates and different volume. The timing, the rate and the volume are not as important as individuals' ability to retain money.

In a particular economy you will see a company where employees come and leave within a very short period. You see an organization where employees work and their minds are somewhere outside that organization. I mean places where you work and what is paramount in your deepest mind is to find an alternative and get out as soon as possible. In such a situation, you will not plan to get your younger brother a job in your organization, all things being equal. But in the same economy you find another company where the employees do not want to leave. They want to grow within that company. Their prayer is to move to the next level within the system.

So many factors could be responsible for the difference. Sometimes, it is the remuneration: salaries, allowances and other benefits. But so many times it is not the money. Even when money is involved, money is not the only factor.

I know a man who retired from Nigerian Ports Authority so many years ago. He was actually affected by the mass retrenchment in the Federal Civil Service carried out as part of right-sizing exercise by the Murtala/Obasanjo Administration around 1975/1976. During a conversation recently, I got to know that before he retired from the Ports Authority, there was a time he and his only two sons were working in the same Ports Authority. If he helped his two sons to be employed in that same organization, imagine how many relatives and friends he must have brought to the organization. What was he bringing them for? They should come and enjoy and benefit from the goodness of the Nigerian Ports Authority. Working in that organization must have been so attractive.

The point here is that there is a way you will engage the money in your hands that it will certainly attract to you its types. That is the only area where the saying that "it takes money to make money" is applicable. It takes the money you have to make the money you need. The amount or volume is irrelevant. The good news is that there is nobody who does not have money no matter how small. At least there is no adult that does not touch money a day or a week or at worst in a month. That is all you need to turn your financial situation around. The money you do not have and could not get is the money you do not need, at least for now. Stop bothering yourself about what you lack. Think about what you have and what you can do with it. Early in life I have come to the conclusion that "whatever I cannot afford is what I can avoid". And what I can afford changes with time, so also what I can avoid.

There is a saying in my native place that **'money is a visitor'**. Our people also say that when that visitor comes to you, ensure you do something with it. They say that because of their experience with many people who have had money or pretended to have money at sometime, but later obviously became broke. And usually such people become broke for life. Very many in our society believe this saying. But many people, including those who sing daily, that 'money is a visitor' are not always able to keep that visitor each time it comes to them.

Whether or not I believe money is a visitor is not the issue. The point we need to get is that money comes to all of us at certain time or the other. We also need to know that it is more important to know there are things we can do to make the flow of money a permanent thing in our direction.

MONEY FLOW

In every economy, there is the flow of money. The flow of money can also be called the flow of wealth or resources. Governments all over the world are busy controlling and directing the flow of money. Good governance is about directing the money flow within the economy, the commonwealth, in the way it will benefit the large majority of the citizens and residents.

Corporate businesses, agencies of government and individual business people all over the world are busy trying to influence the direction of money flow. That is business wisdom. It is financial intelligence. They do everything possible to ensure money flows in their direction. Or at least they do everything to know the direction money is flowing and then position themselves or their organizations in such direction. Wealthy economies and developed nations are what they are because they have been able to properly influence the flow of money within their economies and from outside their economies to their national advantage.

The point is, money is always there. It will always flow, in the right or the wrong direction. Wealthy nations are not necessarily those with more money available to them than others. They are those who have succeeded in directing the available resources in the direction that will benefit the majority. As an individual and as a beginner, you may not have the power to influence the direction money flows. Of course, you do not control the national budget. You do not make the tax laws. You do not make the business and company laws in your state. And these are fundamental factors that influence the flow of money within an economy. But you can position yourself in the direction the money flows.

There are always what to do for money to flow in your direction. Instead of mourning the direction money flows, do things that will make it flow in your direction. Less I forget to mention this: Money flows in the direction of services. It flows in the direction of value creation. It flows in the direction of problem solving. Money flows in the direction of selfless services. This principle is both spiritual and economic. It has both intrinsic and extrinsic applications.

DOUBLE PERSONALITY OF MONEY
Money is like man himself. Man is physical and spiritual at the same time. Man is external and internal at the same time. That is why it is possible for me to make the loudest noise, a show of strong beliefs and commitment about something, but on the inside of me I do not believe in that thing. In fact, it is possible I actually believe the opposite. That means I have applied my external person to that thing, for whatever reason, but my internal person is actually against it. It is possible for me to appear as your best friend while internally I am your worst enemy. Man can actually reflect double personalities at the same time.

Money has intrinsic nature and extrinsic nature. It has both intrinsic form and extrinsic form. Extrinsic is external, intrinsic is internal. You need to understand the two forms. People who understand the intrinsic form and value of money will always attract money. Henry Ford once made bold to say that **if all his wealth is taken away from him one day, within a very short time he would build more wealth**. The truth is that you can only take away the extrinsic wealth from a man, but you cannot take the intrinsic wealth from someone that has it. Except where the man himself has done or is doing things that drive value away.

The intrinsic is attached to the man himself. It is in his mind. It is in his thought. It has to do with his reasoning, value system and decision making.

And you know what? The real money is intrinsic; the extrinsic is just the result. Of course, you can sometimes get the extrinsic without the intrinsic. The truth is that the extrinsic without the intrinsic will not last. The extrinsic wealth is looking for its intrinsic equivalent, the real wealth. Wherever it finds the intrinsic, the extrinsic will stay and multiply there.

EXTERNAL CONTRADICTION
As strong as this principle of intrinsic and extrinsic value of money is, there are thousands of people in our society who try hard to break the rules. In the end, they get themselves broken rather than breaking the principle. Even where they seem to have succeeded on the short run, the principle has always prevailed on the long run.

KNOWLEDGE IS POWER: PLANNING IS PROGRESS

There are three similar stories that came to my mind as I think on how the principle will always prevail. I will like to use them to illustrate the fact that one can only pretend for a while:

1. The president of Nigeria was scheduled for state visit to a state in the south eastern zone of the country some years ago. The normal thing is that the governor of the state will list all the projects he has executed for the president to commission. Of course, there was no law that says the president must commission state projects. However, this practice which has become a standard among the states is an honor to both the president and the governor. On this occasion, one of the projects listed was the street light projects in a particular senatorial zone in the state. To the surprise of the governor and other stakeholders, the project was not completed even as at the early morning of the president visit.

To avoid embarrassment, an arrangement was made to connect the street light to a hired generating set in order to show that the project was successfully executed. The project was commissioned, the street was lit throughout the two days of the presidential state visit. The streets remain bright for some days after the commissioning event. Many unsuspecting residents were happily commending the state government for a job well done. To their amazement, by the end of the following week the streets went dark again. The project was never completed during the administration of the governor and I am not sure the subsequent government ever attempted to continue with the street light project again. The fact is that many of the citizens and residents got to know that there was no street light in the first place.

2. There was also a popular story of a state government that spent huge sums from the state budget to execute a poultry project. There was actually no poultry project. This governor also ended up hiring an abandoned poultry facility, clean up and decorated the place. He then rented thousands of birds to fill the place for the commissioning by the president. On the long run, the truth became a public knowledge.

3. Another state governor was in the habit of deceiving people with rural water borehole projects. Whereas, they only erected overhead tanks and contracted tanker operators to fill the tanks with water. Today many of those tanks, taps and the purported boreholes are nowhere to be found. Some of them you can only see signboards in the bush to show that there was an attempt to do a project in that place some years ago.

The life span of lie is very short.

WHEN THE TRUTH RETURNS
There are so many people who live in affluence today who every discerning mind knows the money will leave them in a matter of time. I see a lot of them every day. There are many wealthy people today that their money can never last to their next generation. This is not a curse; it is the reality of life. It has to do with habit, attitude and possession of right or wrong knowledge. Many of the richest people in our society few years ago have their children and grand children living in penury today.

The good news is, when that money leaves them it will not return to heaven, it will look for people who understand the intrinsic reality of money and stay with them. Of course, Henry Ford did not only sustain his wealth for a life time, his wealth is still growing about a century after his death. That is the power of intrinsic wealth.

INCREASE BY DECREASING

There is a particular portion of the Bible that can also help to drive home this point. "**There is one who scatters, yet increases more; And there is one who withholds more than is right, But it leads to poverty**" Proverbs 11:24

The impulse of this portion is that spending does not reduce money or wealth. It is wrong spending that brings poverty. In fact, right spending is what creates wealth. I do not know many other things in life that increase by reducing. Later in this book we will discuss on how to spend money. Money in your hand can increase by spending it right. This is an unbeatable principle of life.

That tells you there is more to money than what you see physically. I am not talking of the spiritual dimension of money. And I will not want to go into such. This is because an average African will jump at that? Africans believe more in the spiritual. Especially because many of us believe that the spiritual is what we cannot control. And so, we can always exonerate ourselves and blame the unseen forces for our poverty.

I want to talk on those things that are right within your control.

Attract the intrinsic, the extrinsic will naturally run after you. Get the power to make money and money must come to you. Build the personality that attracts money, cultivate the habit of **'value add'** or **'value creation'**. Learn to spend well the little you have and much will follow after you. Acquire knowledge and information about wealth creation. Apply the knowledge and money becomes naturally available to you. Learn to save from the little you have and it will naturally multiply in your hands.

BUSINESS AND INFORMATION

To know what business to do, you need information. To know how to do it successfully and profitably you need information. If you want to revive a dyeing business you need information on how to do that. When you are looking for money to start your business, you need information on how to raise money. There are times that competition and competitors become the major obstacle to your business growth and you need to tackle the competitors creatively. In order to do this, you need information about your competitors and about the market in general. You need to look for information that your competitors have about the business or the industry. Hence, it can be said that information is business. After you have had an idea of what to do, you need enough information on how to do it.

In fact, if you don't have the right information, you will not even have the ideas of what business to do. Buy books on the area of your interest and ensure you read them. Listen to television and radio programs relevant to your area of interest. Read newspapers and magazines. Attend seminars with good attention. If you see your mate is doing better than you are doing, he probably knows something you don't know.

LEARN PURPOSEFULLY
No one has all the time to do all he may want to do at any particular time. For this reason, you will need to develop an area of interest on which you will concentrate looking for information. Do you know the reason why everyone who goes to school (Higher Institutions) must of a necessity select an area of study or specialization?

Have you ever asked why all undergraduates don't do the same course in the University? By facing a particular area or industry, you gain opportunity to know more and deeper about that particular area of study. That will make for digging deep into that area. The more you know about the business you are doing or about to do, the better you will do in it. Know your customers, know your market, and know your competitors and their secrets. Know about the future of the business you are about to do. Anytime you are failing in business, always assume there is something you need to learn to succeed. Learn a better way to doing that thing.

EXPLORE NEW AREAS
Much as you will need to specialize, concentrate and get committed to a particular area of business, you need to create a little time to look at those areas that are new and strange to you. There may be better opportunities there.

INVESTING IN KNOWLEDGE
Acquiring good knowledge will usually cost you money, time

KNOWLEDGE IS POWER: PLANNING IS PROGRESS

and energy. Whatever you use to buy knowledge is not a waste, it is an investment. The best investment is the investment in your brain. That is where your value comes in. You cannot invest on something you don't have value for. If I see your budget or your expenses record, I can tell your value and predict your financial and career future.

How much of your current income do you invest in gaining new knowledge? I have personally invested above a million naira in acquiring new knowledge within the first three quarters of this year. I will still invest more in the last quarter. I will not tell you what percentage of my annual income this is. But I am sure there are many of my mates that will earn five hundred percent of my annual income and will not buy or read one new book a year. I pay for executive courses on my own. I buy books on different topics on different aspects of life. I buy tapes and listen to them while in traffic in the car. I attend seminar and also invest in academic activities.

You know what? These are guaranteed investments. The money will always come back. One guaranteed way to **increase your earning** is to **increase your learning**. When you know better you will live better. This is a principle of life. It works for individuals and the society at large. Many who are complaining about lack of capital to start business are people who are not sincere to themselves. Knowledge is power. Money answers to the right knowledge. When knowledge talks, money must run. All of us pay for our ignorance. And everyone has an area of ignorance. We all pay for our ignorance to the one that has the right knowledge. We pay doctors for what they know about our health that we don't know ourselves. When you know what others don't know, they will pay you for it, directly or indirectly.

IT DOES NOT COST A FORTUNE
I must say this; it does not always cost a fortune to acquire the right knowledge. Often times, it is the mode of learning that actually cost much, because, the mode of learning most times has some status or level content. There are times you have a choice between University of Lagos and Harvard Business School. Your choice has cost implication and most times, it does have more to do with status than the quality of knowledge. There are, of course, some differences in the quality of learning. But they are not such that you cannot make up for. And who says you cannot go to Harvard after your have profitably applied what you learnt from University of Lagos.

Whatever level you are, you can always afford the knowledge you desperately need, as long as you are sincere to yourself. What someone is learning in the class, the other person can learn in the street. The man in the class will later need to come to the street for the practical. If you cannot buy, you can borrow. To crown it all, there is enough free useful information about virtually any subject in the world today. This is particularly with the advent of internet. That may be all you need to start with.

There are many important questions about money making and personal development that you can ask other people for free. You will get useful answers especially if they are sure you are serious about it. Free information will not always be enough, but it will take you a long way until you will be able to afford the one you must pay for.

POWER OF PLANNING

It is normal for you to have good and profitable ideas without the needed physical resources to transform your idea into reality. The truth is that every great idea has embedded in it the needed resources to bring it to reality. All it requires is good planning. Good planning, because good ideas grow and pass through a process to maturity. As it grows, it unlocks the resources to execute each stage of its growth. The resources available at a particular stage must be identified, properly planned and utilized for maximum profitability.

The only sure vehicle that will get you from where you are to where you want to be is planning. Even the best idea is useless until it translates to reality and results. To transform idea to result requires planning. Without prejudice to the definition of planning in our managerial economics and fundamentals of management, I will simply define planning as **step by step definition of actions that will take you to your desired result or end. It also means specific definition and selection of alternatives**. You remember Economics was defines as the **'study of relationships between ends and scarce means which have alternative uses'**.

The means are always there, even though they are scarce. The scarcity is not the problem. Selection of alternatives has always been the problem. It is planning that helps you select the right alternative use for the scarce means or resources.

PLANNING FOR MAXIMUM SUCCESS
In business, there is nothing like luck, what you have in business is planning. Failure to plan is planning to fail.

From the beginning, you must be planning to position yourself for success. Success or failure in life is certainly determined by the ability to plan and execute the plan or lack of it.

PERSONAL ECONOMIC PLANNING
When we talk of wealth creation, we talk of economy. Remember the definition of economics in your college days. Economics is the **social science, which studies human behavior as a relationship between ends and scarce means, which have alternative uses.** Ends are always very numerous but means are always very scarce. Ends are your needs, desires and expectations.

Means are the resources available to achieve them. Planning is about the relationship between ends and means. Selection of the right alternative is the key to any legitimate success. And selection of alternative is largely controlled by human behavior, that is, our values, priorities and mind set. It is controlled by our perception, by our emotions and actions motivated by such emotions.

IDENTIFYING YOUR ENDS
Ability to properly identify your desired ends motivates you to be able to plan for them. Human needs are basically similar. The only difference is that some are able to identify their needs, express those needs, plan to get them met and

ultimately got them met. Others hide their needs, pretend not to have needs, have no plan to meet the needs and never get their needs met. Those are people that look for other people to blame for their lack and poverty. There are others who simply live their lives mourning the fact that they were born into the world where there are not enough resources available to meet their needs.

On daily basis, I meet people who tell me they would have done some wonderful things if only they had money. Depending on the situation, but I frankly tell some of them that they can never have the money. That is absolute truth. Stop bothering about what you will do if you have money. Since you don't have the money look for what you can do without money. And there are many good, legitimate and productive things you can do without money.

Nature does not guarantee that everybody will have money at a particular time. Nature only guarantees everyone has something that can be put to productive use at a particular time. Very many pick offence and they remain the way they are. A few others take time to think about it and decide to take the way of planning and becoming productive with whatever they have. The difference is always clear after sometime.

I may need to repeat this! If there is nothing productive you can do without money, then that money to do something will never come to you. This is because money only comes by doing something productive. It is resourcefulness that attracts resources not the other way round. If there is nothing you can do with the little you have, that much you are waiting for will never come. Of course, there is always something you can do. There is something you can do with what you have because there is nobody that lacks everything; at least there is something you have. The problem is that many people do not appreciate what they have. The purpose of this book is to make you see and appreciate what you have and with adequate planning put it to productive use. The other side is that there is nobody that has everything. This includes those wealthy and highly placed ones who appear to lack nothing. Everybody has a need or needs. By this means, nature provides ground for exchange of values. You meet my need, I meet your need. No need is superior to the other. And people meeting one particular need cannot be seen to be inferior to those meeting other ones.

Your needs are very important, but it is in meeting other people's needs that you can get your own met. Backward people in life are usually those who allow their needs to dominate them. Wealthy and successful people in life are those who get busy meeting other people's needs. Meeting their own individual needs becomes automatic.

Anybody who waits for money to come before planning how to spend it can never be a good spender. If you wait to become the president of the country before you articulate what to do as a president, you can never be a good president. Every developed society looks for people who already have plans when they want to elect a president or leader. Most backward nations of the world are where someone just got presidency, kingship or leadership bestowed on him for whatever reason.

For you to be able to apply the principles taught in this book, you need to determine your motivation for doing whatever you are doing. Wrong motivation will drain your energy. It will limit your planning ability. Successful planning requires commitment and passion, especially now that we are not talking about planning how to spend the money that is freely available. We are talking of resources that it takes vision to unlock.

By the way you feel and go about your needs, I can determine your major motivation and success potentials. And this will determine your ability to see what others do not see. It will determine how far you can see opportunity where others see adversity. It tells of your ability to see those means that others ignore simply because they allow their needs or ends to dominate them.

THREE LEVELS OF HUMAN NEEDS

1. PRIMARY NEEDS

These are the ends that everybody needs for survival. Even for people who cannot meet these ends, somebody else somewhere must meet these needs for them. Otherwise, such people will not even stay alive or be regarded as human beings. If they remain in the human society at all, they will remain as public nuisance. That is the idea behind social security system in some societies. These primary needs include:
- Food
- Clothing
- Shelter

As important as these needs are, they must not be your major motivation in life.

People who are driven only by these needs usually don't have plan for other things in life. At the same time, they don't get fulfilled in life at the long run. They don't achieve great success or wealth, because they never desire it nor plan for it. They are often not ready to pay the price for building lasting wealth.

Another characteristic of these people is that, if they plan at all, they don't have a long term plan. They are short-term thinkers. In addition, these people's motivation in whatever they do is money, immediate money. Because their thought is all about those things that money can buy. If you get to know that William (Bill) Gates, the richest man in the world today rides a 7 years old car, you will know there is more to having money than personal gratification. As at 2006, Bill Gates was riding a 1999 Mazda car. Warren Buffet, the world's richest investor, still lives today in the house he built in 1959. That will convince you that money is more than just for meeting personal needs. Anything that will not bring money and bring it immediately will not motivate them (People driven, only by primary needs).

People in this primary needs class are not good planners; they are not good investors or entrepreneurs. The maximum they can be are traders. They cannot generate ideas that will solve human problems of food, clothes and shelter. They cannot follow an idea to reality. Do you know someone, who if he can get good food, good cloths and good house for free, he would not even work or plan any more in life? That is an example of people motivated by this level of needs. And every society has a number of people like that.

I remember the story of a young man who said if he could just get seven thousand naira, he would first go and buy 'fufu' (local food made from cassava) to eat before thinking of any other thing. That was about 29 years ago (1985). I think seven thousand naira in 1985 is equivalent of about two to three million naira today. My uncle bought a brand new Peugeot 404 pickup van for eleven thousand naira less than two years before then.

The point is, that was the dominant thought in his mind. A person's dominant thought determines virtually every other thing about him. Anyone dominated by the thought of these trivial things will never have the capacity and courage to dream of things of more consequence and value in life. For you to develop the habit of planning for maximum achievement, you need to think and see beyond the basic or primary needs of life. Never allow these primary needs to dominate you. Never build your values around these primary needs.

The irony of our world is that this is the class that the majority belongs. The most dominant thought in the minds of majority is about what they will eat, what they will put on and where they will live. For many, if these needs are met they will not even do any other thing with their lives. These are people who read only to pass examinations. They go to school only to get jobs. They get jobs only to meet their personal needs.

Of course, these needs are very important. The smart people think more of how they will meet these needs in other people's lives and they automatically meet these and other needs in their own lives.

SECONDARY NEEDS
These will include:
- High level income
- High level of comfort
- Personal security
- Ability to take care of self and family
- Basic health care
- Ownership of home to taste etc.

These are for people who see beyond the primary needs of human beings. They see the secondary needs in addition to the basic primary needs of all men. Their motivation is beyond food, cloth and shelter. Those with mindsets around secondary level of human needs usually plan and pay a lot of price to realize their goals. They are always willing to discipline themselves to achieve what they want. However, these people are always anxious. Money is their major motivation in life, because their needs are all what money can buy. They achieve their ends at the expense of other good things of life like good health, human relation, education and religion. The major difference between these people and the primary needs people is that secondary needs people don't usually get contented with little. They are not satisfied with ordinary survival. Most middle class and average income people belong to this category. Many people who plan their

KNOWLEDGE IS POWER: PLANNING IS PROGRESS

lives on employment, fat salaries and job security are also in this class.

These classes of people are planners, but medium term planners. They plan how to get money but they don't plan how to enjoy the money on the long run. They believe when money comes, every other thing will fall in line. They can sometimes pay any price (including sacrificing human life) to make sure they acquire plenty of money. It is either they don't spend or they over spend.

To these people, money is their end and money is also their means. To be a good planner, to pursue a good idea to a successful end, you must see beyond the secondary human needs. And it is this mindset that will make some of the ideas that this book is teaching make meaning to you. Sometimes, these short term planners never set standards, because they never try what others have not tried; they don't want to take much risk, and they don't want to lose money. They manifest high level of self centeredness. They can sacrifice another human life for their desire to get money and what money can buy. Their problem is that of distorted values.

Many people in this class are those with high technical and professional knowledge in their different fields. But they are also often devoid of general wisdom for living and maximum impact. These people live with high level of entitlement mentality.

TERTIARY NEEDS

These are needs that relate to other values that create long-term happiness. They include:

- Having time for family and friends
- Having the desired and adequate education
- Access to good health care
- Memorable experiences such as travels and tours
- Charitable and philanthropic giving
- Volunteer social services to the society
- Community and national leadership and influence
- Spiritual services and growth.

People who appreciate this level of human needs, in addition to the first two are visionaries; they are good planners and maximum achievers. They usually identify means to achieving good ends which most average people around them will not identify. They have less risk of depression, less anxiety, and high self esteem. They normally have less physical, emotional, behavioral and relationship problems. These people normally score high on the indicator testing of self-actualization and vitality. To them, money is not always the primary goal of their ideas. To them, money is important but money is not always the answer.

It is easier for these people to identify their other means to realize their ideas when money is not yet available. They easily take advantage of other factors like time, knowledge and relationship in starting the execution of their ideas and plans.

The good news is that anyone can decide to change his mind set. You can always change your perception and value. You can change your culture, you can change habit and you can change your behavior. Every habit is formed and can be broken.

On a final analysis, your value system and motivating factor will determine how far you can go in any endeavor.

ABRAHAM MASLOW THEORY OF MOTIVATION
Abraham Maslow was an American Psychologist who was best known for creating Maslow's hierarchy of need, a theory of psychological health predicated on fulfilling innate human needs in priority, culminating in self-actualization.
Maslow (1943) stated that people are motivated to achieve certain needs. When one need is fulfilled a person seeks to fulfill the next one, and so on.

I did the first edition of this book in 2006/2007. As at that time I had never heard about Abraham Maslow or his theory of motivation. I don't know how that happened. I believe I am a young man that is committed to personal development by reading wide. Yet, I never knew about these all-important Maslow theory. It was Pastor Sam. Adeyemi who used the Maslow's theory of human needs for illustration in a series of sermons in 2011. And that was my first time to hear about Maslow and his theory.

To my surprise, my categorization of human needs in line with motivation and personal values in 2007 largely conforms to Maslow's classification of 1943; except that Maslow categorized human needs in five levels as against my three levels. I recommend Maslow's theories of human needs and motivation for further studies. Google will provide you with a lot of information on Maslow and his theory.

IDENTIFYING YOUR MEANS
As earlier stated, planning has to do with establishing an appropriate relationship between ends (needs) and scarce means (resources). Ends are unlimited. Means are always very scarce. And that has been the age long pattern. To properly identify your means is to assure yourself that when money is not yet available, you still have other resources for success. These other resources have the ability to generate money when properly applied. They are also always more available to everyone than money. Anybody who wants to wait for money in Nigeria is not likely going to start any business. Start with what you have.

When the idea of writing this book (first edition) came to me, I knew it was going to cost money. And certainly I did not have all the money involved. However, I had my brain, some related texts on the subject I could consult, a personal computer on my table with internet connection, which will enable me search for necessary information. I also have some contacts and relationships, which I can use to further enrich my knowledge on the subject matter. Definitely, by the time I use all these to develop the project up to the stage of a manuscript, the needed money will surely come. That is the principle.

KNOWLEDGE IS POWER: PLANNING IS PROGRESS

Try it, it works without fail. The same resources I used in putting the materials together would be used in generating the fund. The fact that I have the manuscript already makes securing funds easier. The manuscript becomes the rallying point for other resources.

What is planning here? I arrange all the required resources and put those ones that are not yet available last. When I don't have money, I will not make a plan which the execution will start with money. I put those things that my brain and my spare time can do first. Anytime I want to contact a person or institution for money I must have got something tangible to show them. I show them the work I have done which is packaged in a manuscript. Yours may be in another format. That alone is going to make anybody have confidence in my project.

To be sure, some of your means or resources will include:
- Your time
- Your brain
- Your relationships
- Your location
- Your physical assets or properties
- Your certificate and qualification
- Your past experience and so on
- Then, your money

The ideal thing is to plan to achieve your goals with what you have. The ones you have, use wisely and judiciously, while you plan to get the ones that you don't have with what you have.

Plan your time very well; time is more valuable than money. Avoid any waste of time.

Use your brain very well; it is the greatest resource available to you. Take good care of it, develop it and you will get what you want on the long run. Cherish the relationship you already have, if they are good ones. Take advantage of them to realize your goals, while you consciously develop more profitable relationships. Take advantage of your current location and know when to change your location, based on advantage and disadvantage of such location.

Think of how you can apply some of your personal properties to achieve your goal. Ensure there is no idle capacity; ensure you are not keeping any asset just for the sake of it. Avoid liabilities that people call assets. Anything that is going to take from you more than it is giving you is a liability not an asset. Look for business that you can comfortably and profitably start in your living room, when you cannot afford the luxury of an office accommodation. Find out whether there is any way you can make use of some of your household materials to make money, without any injury to your health or personality.

How about your academic and professional certificates? Think of how better you can use them to make money. I once heard a politician proposing a government program whereby, graduates will be provided with funds to pursue their entrepreneurial ideas as they use their certificates as collateral securities. That will be a very good program that can almost banish unemployment in the country. But the problem is that most of our graduates will never be able pay the money back, because they were not taught like that in the school. They are not equipped to manage resources productively. We were all taught in the school how to look for job. That, coupled with poor infrastructure, will mean that most graduates will not repay such start-up loans

Think of what you can do with your past experiences to generate income. Also think of what you can do with your current income. Don't tell me it is too small. If you are earning ten thousand naira and you cannot save and do something with it, when you start earning one hundred thousand naira you would not do anything serious with it.

Use what you have; you will certainly get what you need.

BUSINESS PLAN
If you are concerned about starting a business or raising capital for your new business, you need a good business plan. A good business plan with great presentation can help you raise all the money you need. A bad business plan with poor presentation can make you lose a lifetime opportunity. Most times the outcome of your business may not be exactly according to the business plan.

Even with that, writing a good plan has enough advantages. According to Robert Kiyosaki, "**the process of creating a business plan with numbers is a process that causes the**

entrepreneur to think through the venture in more detail and then put it down on paper. A successful business is created before there is a business, it starts in the mind. Business plan is that creation process put down on paper".

The plan does not have to be elaborate. Neither does it need involving classical academic work. It can be very simple, at your level. A plan simply lets the potential investor see the thoughts inside the mind of the entrepreneur. Also, it allows the investor to know that you are serious about the proposed business. Your plan must demonstrate your readiness to apply your means (what you have) to the business, it will motivate others to be ready to give their means to your idea.

Always remember that any good idea that comes to you, you have something to donate to make it work. The reason why most people complain of difficulty in raising capital to finance their ideas is that they have not applied the necessary diligence to put their ideas down in the way that will bring money from the pockets of the people who have the money. There is money out there. There are so many people with money but without ideas or with ideas that are less lucrative than yours.

"All men seek one goal: success or happiness. The only way to achieve success is to express your-self completely in the service to the society.

First, have a definite, clear, practical idea – a goal, an objective.

Second, have necessary means to achieve your end, wisdom, money, materials and methods.
Third, adjust all your means to those ends". Aristotle (384BC-322BC)

The power of planning is in the ability to identify your means and adjust them to your ends.

FINANCIAL PROJECTIONS
"**If you are interested about becoming an entrepreneur, an interesting exercise is to hire an experienced Accountant to help you with a proposed budget and cash flow analysis**". If you have approached a bank for loan before, one major thing the banker will demand from you is a financial projection or cash flow analysis. "**The reason this is an important exercise, even if you do not go through the product or the business is that the exercise will give you a better idea of what it costs to start and run a business**". Robert Kiyosaki.

I have stated before that money is not the only thing required in starting a business; it is just one of those things, and is ideally the last thing. A good knowledge of the business you want to do and the ability to communicate your mind will definitely give you the money you need. An important aspect of your plan is the financial projection. Simply put, it is the budget of your idea in monetary terms. It is about what the business will cost you and your expected income from the business. That is expressing your idea in figures.

KNOWLEDGE IS POWER: PLANNING IS PROGRESS

up for the identified weaknesses. Feasibility study is one other thing you can also use the services of an expert to do. The report makes the picture of where you are going clearer to you. Your outcome becomes largely and humanly predictable.

I must say that your business plan does not have to be a complex academic document. This is especially so as you are a beginner. Everybody can do a plan, just like everybody can write a love letter or at least text message to his or her lover. Everybody can do financial projection, just like everybody can write down a list of his expenses and income. If you can think, you can plan. The only difference is that you have to take time to intentionally think through that specific area. Your thought must also be committed to writing. That marks the major difference between a business plan and ordinary thinking or writing.

I have met people who complain about lack of money to actualize their laudable ideas. You will be surprised when you interview these people further. Many have not actually decided about what they want to do. Some don't even know anything specific about what they said they want to do. There are others who have tried to convince me that they actually know what they want to do if only they can see somebody that will give them money. The next question I ask is where is the plan? Of course, for a starter I don't expect a well decorated and bogus academically organized plan. The response, however from very many young people is that I have not written it out or it is in my mind.

And truly you don't expect me to invest in your mind. I cannot

In case you are not good at doing that, always find a way of contacting and engaging an expert. If you have money to do that, good; if not, a portion of your expected income may be promised for the service. Most of the information will come from you based on your knowledge of the business. The expert will translate the information into figures and financial terms.

FEASIBILITY STUDY

This is usually part of a business plan. This is particularly when you are starting a new business or diversifying into a new area. Some people call it feasibility report. The study is actually the process while the report is the result. Feasibility study is about the process of gathering all necessary and available information about the potential success or otherwise of the business you want to do. Here, no item of information is too small. Everything about the business is important.

You obtain information about the product, alternative products, the would-be consumer or customers and their expectation and behavior. You gather information about the location, the culture, the government, the laws and other things that can affect your would be business. Information about likely competitors, the market entry requirement and so on, are all very important. The essence is that from the information you will be able to identify opportunities for success and threats of failure. The process also enables you to measure your preparedness and strength to combat the threats of failure.

In the process, you identify your weaknesses in facing the challenge of likely failure and devise alternatives for making assess your mind but I can assess a documented plan.

THE PLANNERS' PLAN
When I did the first edition of this book, I believed strongly that with a well articulated business plan, your success in business is almost guaranteed. That is still as true today as it was nine years ago. However, this is a general principle. To every principle there is an exception. I have seen enough exceptions since then. People do wonderful plans in this part of the world. Corporate bodies and business men and women spend fortune to prepare business plans, feasibility studies and financial projections.

Yet, about 90% of these businesses fail at the end of the day. Of course, the one without a plan cannot be among 10% that succeed. My observation is that many people do business plan for formality. Others do it to meet some regulatory requirement. Some people think the essence of doing business plan is to be able to raise money from an investor or a bank. Any plan prepared solely for any of these reasons has failed from the beginning.

You must possess your plan and your plan must possess you. The essence of feasibility study is to ensure you have all necessary information for the success of the business. Even when someone else has done the study for you, it is important you listen through or read through. You must ask all necessary questions until you thoroughly digest the details.

Until the plan has become yours it cannot benefit you. The process of owning the plan is as important as the plan itself.

You must baptize yourself in the details of it and have the summary at your finger tips. Even when you have all the money, you still need a good business plan.

USERS OF A GOOD PLAN

1.   The Planner: I remember my experience with one of my younger sisters some years back. She grew up with my aunty in Ivory Cost. She actually went with the aunty as a primary school girl. She has already lived 13 years in Ivory Coast before we discovered that she only completed the primary education and since then she has been doing trading with our aunty. Based on this revelation the family had requested she should return to Nigeria for further education like the rest of us.

Returning to Nigeria my sister was not ready to return to school. I have tried as much as possible to explain to her why she needed to get further education like any of us. To everybody's surprise, my sister would not listen. Then she had to be forced to go to school. Of course, I knew it was not easy to start secondary school at the age of twenty years.

The point I want to make is this. One day my sister was crying and I had to talk to her as usual. It was this time she told me that she was only going to school because of me. I was shocked but then she insisted she was only doing me favor by going to school in line with the family's wishes for her. How far can you go doing somebody favor? Of course she did not go far.

KNOWLEDGE IS POWER: PLANNING IS PROGRESS

Many people prepare business plan because of other parties like the bankers, the regulators and other investors. The number one person that needs the plan is you. **You must own the plan and the plan must own you**. Your experience during the planning process is much more important than the write up itself. That process exposes you. It educates you. It opens your minds to deep details of the business you want to do. That makes all the difference between success and failure.

2.   Investors: By investors we mean people who want their money to work for them. People who want to put their money in your idea for a return. The return could be monetary or other kinds of return. These people are not ready to lose their hard earned money. Therefore you must be able to convince them that your idea is not a money losing venture.

Your business plan is one major way you can communicate to these people. The plan will give them a clear picture of what you want to do with their money and how you intend to reward them. With the technological advancement and enhanced image, it is possible for you to place order for the most expensive things without having to see them physically. You can order machines and equipments based on pictures you see in the brochures or the internet. The fact is that that picture must be clare enough for you to see all the important parts of the machine. Usually, there could be the side view, front view, rear view inner view and so on. It must be clear enough for you to know the machine when you later see it physically. That is exactly what your business plan does for an investor.

3.   **Regulators:** If you want to enter a regulated market, the regulators will want to see your business plan. They do this on behalf of the public and on behalf of the government. I will not want to dwell much on this. This is because, regulated areas are always more complex. They are not usually for people who don't have some money already.

4.   **Bankers:** Your bankers will usually want to see that your business will be able to pay back any money they lend to you. Your plan is one good way they can know this. Again, I will not want to dwell much on this.

5.   **Other Stakeholders:** Every other person that will play important roles in actualizing your plan falls into this category. This may include your employee, your agent or even sometimes your customers. All these people need clear information on their roles and what they should expect in return. The bottom line in all these is that you must be the number one user of your plan.

THE GOOD PLAN
For the fact that some people pretend to have plan just for the sake of it, it is necessary to state some of the things that will assure you as to whether your plan is good or not. I am saying this particularly for people who want a simple, workable plan. For the big institutions who prepare plans and projections to approach banks and investors for funding, usually the investors or the bank have a way of telling you that your plan is not good enough or otherwise. Sometimes, it is by them asking

KNOWLEDGE IS POWER: PLANNING IS PROGRESS

further questions that will probe into your motives and business viability. At other times they tell you your plan is not good enough simply by declining your request.

Even for those complex corporate business plans, the planner must own the plan; it must go beyond just meeting loan or funding requirement.

1. **It must be in writing:** Until your plan is written, it is not a plan. It remains a wish in your mind. And you remember the saying "**if wishes were horses, even beggars will ride**". One thing I can assure you is that wishes are not horses and they will never be. It is only the process of writing that makes your plan clear.

2. **It must be specific:** Your plan must state specifically what you will do to get what. For example, if you have to approach people for assistance, your plan must state clearly how many people you are going to approach. It must be specific on how much you are going to request from each of them. It must also specify alternative outcomes and alternative actions.

If you are approaching five people, you need to think through and state the likely outcome from each of them. Three people may have 50% probability of giving you what you ask while the other two have 80% probability.

In case these probabilities materialized either way, what are the alternative actions you will take? Are you going to approach more people? If you don't have any means of livelihood at present, you naturally don't expect someone from nowhere to just give you a hundred thousand for nothing. But the secret is that it is easier to get ten thousand naira each from ten people than to get hundred thousand naira from one person. If you don't have any money, at least you have the spare time to move from place to place approaching people. You can approach as many as a hundred persons. Usually you will get at least ten persons that will respond and grant your request. You must state what you will give as an attraction to each of these people.

3. **It must be measurable:** Your plan must be measurable. That is, you must cut it into sizes that could be measured. It must be possible for you to know when you are achieving each item on the plan. If you have planned to visit ten persons a day, it must be possible for you to come back at the close of each day and compare how many people you planned to meet and how many you actually met.

You must allocate time to each of your planned actions. You must allocate other resources as well, if they are available. This is the only way you can measure your progress. It also helps you to measure your level of commitment to actualizing your plan.

4. **Nothing for nothing:** Every part of your plan must clearly identify what you want to achieve at each stage. It must also state what exactly you will do or give to achieve such.

Even though this is the second edition of this work, I have how many chapters I plan to work on per week. I also have how many hours I will give to the work per week. Of course, I have specific other things I intend to sacrifice to be able to meet my target.

One thing is to reduce the number of hours I sleep per week until this project is complete. Another thing is to reduce my attendance at social functions. I had intended starting another Master Degree this year. But I have just sacrificed the Master Degree for this project.

Most people who complain of lack of money are people with a lot of spare time. I know a lady that wakes up most days of the week by ten o'clock in the morning. She told me herself. This same person told me wonderful things she would do if only she has money. The minimum amount of money she needed is over one million naira. The truth is that she has a lot of spare time. She just forgot that **'time is money'**. Good planning will help you to see idle capacity you can convert into productive use. Usually, every poor person has spare time or at lease can create one.

5.   It must be achievable: You must plan for what is achievable. What is achievable is relative and is a function of a lot of things. What is achievable for you will certainly be different from what is achievable for me. "**Life is in stages and men are in sizes**". Your stage in life and your level on the economic ladder is an important factor of what is achievable to you. Another factor is your level of commitment and preparedness. This has to do with what you are ready to do or give in achieving your objectives of realizing your plan.

The bottom line is that what you plan to do at a particular time must not be too big that even you cannot believe it is possible. The moment you don't have that faith in it, you have marked the plan for failure from day one. Too big plans have a way of discouraging you from the onset. Wisdom demands you cut it into achievable sizes. When you achieve one, the joy of your achievement will give you energy to pursue the next one. **Learn to be optimistic and at the same time be realistic**.

6.   Cost Benefit: Your plan must emphasize a cost benefit pattern. Every milestone in the plan has a cost attached to it. At that point the benefit of achieving that milestone must be clearly stated. It is the benefit that is clearly stated that motivates you or any other person to pay the price. For you to state what you want to achieve without properly stating the benefit of achieving it is like asking somebody to work hard for 30 days without a promise of salary at the end of the month.

You must clearly state how you will reward yourself for achieving what you plan. You must state how every other person who plays any role in achieving your objective will be rewarded. An investor wants to know how much or what percentage of return he would get on his money. A banker wants to agree what rate of interest and how you will pay it. Is it monthly, quarterly or annually? An employee or agent wants to know his remuneration and how such will be paid. Even you! You need a solid promise of reward to keep you motivated and committed.

Currently, I am working on four different books. There are specific things I will reward myself with if I am able to achieve specific targets. Your reward depends on your person and your current circumstance. To somebody, it may be a new car. To someone else it may be another thing. The point is that this must be part of your plan and you should be committed to it just as you are committed to any other parts of the plan.

PLAN B
Never try to avoid risks. Instead, plan to take risks and make provision for how to reduce the effect of the risk on you. One major way of doing that is having an alternative plan always at hand. That is, what to do next in case what you intend to do fails. That is why you are better off if you have more than one sources of income.

POWER OF COMMUNICATION AND THE PLACE OF CONNECTION

4

Business is communication and communication is business. If there is anything that you must learn to be successful in the business world, it is the art of communication. To pass your idea to people, you need to be able to communicate well. Any idea that cannot be communicated for people's benefit is certainly useless.

As an inventor, in bringing your discovery to the form that will benefit man, you need some people. Henry Ford had the great idea of manufacturing a six-cylinder engine. He had to gather his team of engineers, give instruction on how they will bring to reality what he had in his mind. Inability to communicate his idea would mean the natural death of that idea. The only way you can make others become part of your idea is by communication. Their participation may be to provide finance, business advice or to work for you as employees. It may even be for you to secure government regulatory and legal approval

We are in the world of people. The business is for the people, the product is for them and the service is for them. You must be able to make them think your own way. As a manager, you must be able to communicate your ideas to your subordinates.

The first lesson a child learns is how to communicate. The first thing he does on arrival to the world is to communicate his feelings, at least by crying. We learn communication throughout our school days, primary to the university. Ironically, a lot of us feel that at graduation we have learnt enough in the area of communication. And that is one major reason why businesses fail and most profitable ideas do not see the light of the day.

As said earlier, on planning, identify your means and arrange them to achieve your ends. Art of communication is one of those means and it is central. You need to learn basic business communication before you look for money or capital. Communication is one of the tools you need to raise the money you require for business. A good communicator will easily raise money or any other resources for his idea.

KNOWLEDGE AND COMMUNICATION
Knowledge and communication are like twin brothers, they go together. Ability to communicate what you know is a proof that you actually know that thing. Until you can communicate

it you have not known it enough. Mind you, I am not talking of communication jargons, as one will need to study in the university. The ability to communicate is right on the inside of all of us; you only need to develop your own. Here, your communication technique depends on your audience and you.

Another relationship between communication and knowledge is that knowledge helps you to communicate. If you know well of what you want to do, you will be able to communicate it. Knowledge gives confidence and to communicate properly you need confidence. Business starts in the mind; communication helps to bring it to the material form.

COMMUNICATION: THE ART OF MARKETING
A marketer is a communicator. It is not only physical product that one markets, you market services, and you market ideas. It is the idea that sells that is profitable. Until it is marketable, it will certainly bring no benefit whatsoever. Learning to market your idea is the key; it is as important as creating the ideas. Communication, here, is the marketing of your idea.

POWER OF CONNECTION
Connection and communication are much related. In communication, the idea or the product or service is the focus. You communicate your idea while you connect yourself. Connection has to do with you not your idea.

Dr. Orji Uzor Kalu, former Governor of Abia State, Nigeria said, "**your ability to know the decision maker, whether he**

POWER OF COMMUNICATION AND THE PLACE OF CONNECTION

is behind the scene or in the open is key to success". That explains the power of connection. Don't forget, connection is about you while communication is about your idea or product. And both of them are about people. Business is all about people.

Communication is marketing while connection is networking. However, one helps the other. A good communicator will easily get connected, all things being equal. A well-connected person will usually communicate boldly. The two are central to business success. If I have an idea, what I do is to start seeking the right connections that will make my idea come true. Good connection sometimes also helps to develop good ideas through interaction.

CONNECTION AND CHARACTER
If I ask anybody, what is the most important thing you need to start your own business or grow your existing business? An average person will answer 'money'! Experience has however proved the contrary. Good character gives good connection; good connection gives you all the money you need. Know it that there are people out there who are looking for honest people they can commit their idle cash to. Banks look for borrowers very seriously. Without lending they cannot continue in business. At least, in order to fulfill their objective of accepting deposit and lending to people or organizations, they must lend. But they are not going to give depositors' money to people of no character or people who are not rightly connected.

POWER OF COMMUNICATION AND THE PLACE OF CONNECTION

In an economy like Nigerian, there is more money outside the banking system. Experts report stated recently that only about 40 million Nigerians put their money in the banks, out of over 160 million people! That is the reason why banks now engage in huge promotional and marketing activities, just to improve our banking culture.

There is money outside there, but men and women of character have access to it. It is character of the borrower that gives the lender the confidence to release his hard earned money. The character we are talking about here is not that of an angel. No. Let your 'yes' be 'yes' and your 'no' be 'no'. Never make promises you are sure you will not be able to fulfill, no matter the pressure. When you must fail an appointment, always try to apologize immediately you become aware of the failure.

I was discussing with one of my consultancy clients few years ago; he needed a loan of about 2 million naira from the bank to boost his business capacity. My intention was to write a loan proposal that will help him get what he wanted. But I had to interview him first, especially as regards his credit history. He told me he had collected loans from two different banks in the past and he paid to terms on each occasion. That point alone can facilitate a speedy approval of his request by any good banker.

Get character, character will give you connection and connection will give you all the money you need. As you work on your character, you are already building your business. On the long run it will pay off. Character is not a matter of religion, it is a personal choice. It doesn't just happen, you develop it. Don't allow the desire to get money take character from you; don't allow it to give you bad character. Of course, bad character will also get you connected, but to the bad people.

In the business world, character is money. It carries the intrinsic value of money. It is called **'social capital.'**

WHY THE RICH GET RICHER
It has been proved with enough evidences that the rich in any society are always getting richer. This is an obvious fact. Jeb Bush once said of **"what it meant for his business career that he was the son of an American president and the brother of an American president and the grandson of a wealthy Wall Street banker and US senator"**. Jeb himself was a Governor of Florida for eight years. His brother George Bush was Governor of Texas for about six years before becoming the US president in 2001.

Although it is not like that at all times. There are actually people who were at one time rich but are very poor today. There are people that were popular years back, but today the reverse is the case.

This is not however to contradict the general knowledge that the rich are getting richer, that the highly placed people in government or any level of the society will always continue in the high places. The latter is rather a confirmation of the former. The secret of the rich getting richer is the relationship or connection they use their riches to purchase. The few ones who fail to use their first fortune to purchase the right connection are those who usually go into oblivion.

Only five minutes telephone conversation with the man that matters may mean more than a million naira or dollars.

HOW CONNECTED YOU ARE
You may not be as connected as Mr. President. Not everybody will have that level of connection. You don't even need such. A lot of people believe that until they know all the 'who-is-who' in the society, they cannot succeed in business. This belief is absolutely wrong.

All you need is to make the conscious efforts of getting connected more and more day by day. Know that the connection you have today is sufficient for today's success. Start at the point where you are, take advantage of that which you have now. Then as a principle, ensure that your connection grows with your business. If getting the right connection is part of your core values, it will reflect in your spending and your use of time.

CONNECTING LIKE A POLITICIAN
Observe the way most successful politicians go about it, their strategies. They nurse the idea into maturity before they declare their intention. Most of them develop themselves and create the needed reputation and popularity while they are still on their first job or employment. He may first plan how to generate enough wealth to pursue his ambition later in life. Then he uses the wealth to create good name for himself in whatever way he could do that.

POWER OF COMMUNICATION AND THE PLACE OF CONNECTION

Start where you are. Start with what you have. Create the needed connection for the business you plan to go into later. Most of the things I do today are the things I have planned as far back as five years. And from the word go I have used every opportunity to create the needed impression and connection. Even when I needed people to guarantee me for bank loan, it was a matter of hours; I was able to produce two reputable personalities, without prior notices.

Think about all the opportunities you have to do that. Your current job may be the best place to start creating good impression of yourself. You meet a number of people daily, create good rapport with them, especially those you know may matter to your future. Take note that every relationship has to be on merit. There are some people that separating from them is the best for now. You have to know those people too and give gap. However, it does not make for enmity or permanent separation; you may still need some of them badly tomorrow.

Have a good diary of telephone numbers. Take proper care of complementary cards. Don't joke with contacts, postal and email addresses; they may mean more than a million naira someday.

DON'T WAIT TO BE CONNECTED. GET CONNECTED

In case you think you don't have the needed connection for business purpose, that should not stop you from starting your own business. There are still some other things you have at

POWER OF COMMUNICATION AND THE PLACE OF CONNECTION

hand, start with them. At least, you have an idea, opportunity, knowledge and possibly some money. Start at that point. With the right attitude and intention, you will grow connection along the line. As you get connected, the journey becomes smoother.

POWER OF OPPORTUNITY

5

The most important thing on the road to success is opportunity. Opportunity is in everything, including adversity, failure, and disappointments. All of them come with certain amount of opportunity. Everything is in opportunity, including money, connection, knowledge and ideas. There is opportunity to get money; people who take advantage of it become rich. There is opportunity to get connected; people who seized it become connected. There is opportunity to get knowledge; people who use it do get knowledge. There is opportunity to get idea; people who use it do get ideas. The list is endless.

A major difference between the rich and the poor is the ability to take advantage of opportunities. The rich man is rich

POWER OF OPPORTUNITY

because he took advantage of opportunity or opportunities, positive or rich because he takes advantage of positive or negative opportunities. He does not only wait for opportunity but he carefully search for it. The poor man is poor because he ignores or misuses opportunity. He does not look for opportunity either. The poor man Father hope for luck than position for opportunity.

Nobody is poor because of lack of opportunity. We don't have equal opportunities in life but everybody has enough opportunity to make him what he wants to be in life. At least, these opportunities would be available to all of us at different times of our lives:

- Ø Opportunity to be creative and generate ideas
- Ø Opportunity to learn and have knowledge
- Ø Opportunity to plan for the future
- Ø Opportunity to communicate your ideas and thoughts
- Ø Opportunity to get connected to the right people
- Ø Opportunity to make choice and make it right
- Ø Opportunity to make money and be rich
- Ø Opportunity to identify your talents, develop them and use them
- Ø Opportunity to invest
- Ø Opportunity to create other opportunities and so on.
- Ø All of these are available to all men at different levels of life and in different dimensions. Look around, you are surrounded by opportunities. And that is what you need to rise to the top.

OPPORTUNITIES ARE NOT MONOPOLIZED
"No man is kept poor because opportunity has been taken away from him; because other people have monopolized the wealth, and have put a fence around it. You may be shut off from engaging in business in certain lines but there are other channels open to you."

You may not have opportunity to go into that lucrative business you admire. There is always another area where an opportunity is open to you. All you need is to take advantage of that. Any opportunity well utilized will create more opportunities.

At different periods, the tide of opportunity sets in different directions, according to the needs of the whole and the particular stage of social evolution, which has been reached. At a time in America, it was industry, production, mechanization, engineering and so on. At that time, being in that cycle almost automatically positioned someone for wealth and riches. At least it provided opportunity enough for anyone in that cycle to live comfortably.

At another time, it was the financial sector that controlled the fortunes in the society. It latter went to agriculture and allied industries, then to marketing and so on. The same cycle is followed in any economy. Nigerian economy is not different. At a time in Nigeria being in the military was a fast way to riches. Some years ago, securing a job in one of the commercial banks guaranteed a comfortable life for a young person. At another time, it was being in the oil and gas industry. Holding a political office is very attractive

nowadays, whether you are in appointive or elective office.
To think that this cycle suggests lack of opportunity to some people or to a sector is a fallacy. The cycle does not discriminate. It allows anybody who is willing and, of course, anybody can join the cycle. There is abundance of opportunity for a man who will go with the tide, instead of trying to swim against it. Information and communication technology sector is very lucrative today in Nigeria and the whole world. Communication today is indisputably very lucrative, and everybody is free to tap his own portion of wealth available in the sector.

I must also add that there are usually other untapped areas in every economy. The richest people will be people who can locate such areas before others will see it. To discover such an area requires creativity which everyone has or at least can develop.

PERSONAL AND SOCIETAL OPPORTUNITY
Opportunity comes to a generation; it comes to a nation and to a community. Opportunity presents itself to an organization or corporate entity. There are companies that have operated profitably for over a century while others close down within five years of existence. There are communities that are well developed while some neighboring communities are backward. There are developed nations as there are those that are less-developed. The difference is in opportunity. Some were wise enough to identify and take advantage of opportunities while others were sleeping.

The same principle applies to individuals. Opportunity comes to all of us, but what we do with opportunity is what matters. In fact, the societal opportunity is always a collection of opportunities for individuals in that society. Developed nations are those with citizens and residents who take advantage of opportunity. Every government program, good or bad, provides some level of opportunity for people who can identify and use it. Look around, you will see people who took advantage of the long years of military rule in Nigeria and made it to the top. Not all of them are crooks, not all of them are rogues. Even many of them only took advantage of the high level of poverty that existed in the country at that time to make their own fortune. They only provide products and service within a less regulated regime and they made their fortune.

UNLIMITED OPPORTUNITIES
The fact that a man wasted an opportunity in the past does not mean another will never come to him. Opportunity is available as sunshine and rain fall, and it keeps coming. As long as we have life, opportunity will keep coming. You may not get the exact opportunity you once lost. But other opportunities will come your way. There is no need regretting the past. There are enough opportunities in the front that you need not looking at the back. Your only reference to the past opportunities is to learn from them and nothing more.

Annulment of the June 12, 1993 election in Nigeria was a major historical event and setback in the Nigerian political landscape. Yet, it became a very huge enterprise which some people capitalized on to find relevance in the Nigerian economy and the world stage. There are many in Nigerian politics today who would have remained in oblivion except for their participation in the agitation for the revalidation of the June 12 mandate.

Many people who became governors, senators and honorable members at the return of democracy in 1999, especially from the south-western part of the country, were people who became known simply because of their roles in the June 12 struggle. Whether all of these people actually believed that much in democracy, fairness and rule of law is another question entirely. The point is that they saw opportunity in that event and grabbed it, even in those dark days of the military dictatorship.

HOW TO IDENTIFY OPPORTUNITY
It is good you know what you are looking for; in case you meet it on the way you will be able to recognize it. The road of life is littered with opportunities; only the wise will identify and use them.

How then do you Identify Opportunity?
1. **By Inspiration:** God created all men and we all have intuitions. Ideas drop into our hearts, good or bad. Most of them carry opportunity. When thoughts drop into your heart, don't ignore them, except you are sure they are bad ones. Jot them down for further thought and analysis. Read about them, ask questions about them. Your analysis will most likely bring out opportunity yet unidentified.

2.   By Thoughtfulness: Everybody thinks, but not everybody is thoughtful. The thoughtful man is the one that controls his thought. He decides what he wants to think about and the direction of his thought. Take specific topic, area of life or event. Think critically about it, you are likely going to find opportunity hidden to other people. Think about specific human and societal problems. Think about it as if the solution must be within reach and not as someone mourning your personal or societal condition. All invention in human history came from people thinking and asking question about human problems, and how to solve them.

3.   By Observation: Develop the attitude of not just seeing but observing. Always look thoughtfully. Ask yourself questions on what you see. Observation is not the same as looking. Observation is looking and thinking at the same time.

4.   **Through Discomfort or Dislike:** Inside that entire thing called failure or misfortune is a big opportunity. Each time you are confronted by a difficult situation, look for the opportunity that situation can offer. Opportunity is always in adversity. That problem that is bothering you may be an indication that you can discover the solution. Be positive about it. Think about it with an open mind. You will be surprised at what you may come out with.

OPPORTUNITY IN ADVERSITY
To somebody who knows the power of opportunity, there is nothing like failure or set back. All of them come with opportunity.

That you lost your job or never got one is an opportunity to become your own boss. Employ yourself.

That you are poor is an opportunity for you to learn how to turn poverty to riches. That you don't have capital is an opportunity for you to learn how to start a business without capital. The childhood experience of Robert Kiyosaki with his poor and rich fathers has provided him the opportunity to learn all the details of how to create and build wealth. Today, he is not only a blessing to America but to the whole world in the area of entrepreneurship and wealth creation.

The scourge of HIV/AIDS is a deadly blow on this entire generation, yet it has provided opportunity for thousands of people to become millionaires. The same is applicable to malaria, tuberculosis and the likes. Think about it. There is a seed of benefit in every adversity.

THE THREE LAWS OF MONEY

6

WHAT YOU SHOULD KNOW ABOUT MONEY

The most important subject which is not taught in schools is how to make money. To some of us that read Accounting, we were thought about money but not about how to make money. We learned how to manage money for other people. Generally, the school taught us how to serve other people. We were taught how to express the financial process in financial and economic language. What actually creates money is more than just reporting and projection. It is the thought process that leads to specific pattern of decisions and actions that creates money or wealth. And that is what the formal school does not teach. There is

THE THREE LAWS OF MONEY

nothing wrong in serving other people, but that must not be the end of the story. He that serves must also be served one day.

I have come to discover that if you have hope of being served one day, you will likely serve better and serve carefully. That is one of the major reasons why great leaders don't joke with succession planning. That hope makes the servant to put himself in the master's shoes often times. Hence, the school that only teaches only how to serve is not doing the best to its products. We were all made to believe there is job outside there that we would do when we graduate. Even when the reality is telling us the contrary, our line of thought has been patterned along that line and has become difficult to change. We must start to face the reality, start learning how to make money.

Essentially and in my own opinion, there are three basic lessons about money:
1. How to make money
2. How to save money
3. How to spend money

The more of these lessons you learn and practice the more successful you will be financially. As long as a man ignores these basics, he continues to be in want.

VALUE FOR MONEY
When you have value for money, money will come to you. A

lot of people will never want to identify with the importance of money in their lives, especially if you are from an area like my own native place. Some, out of religion even claim not to like money. I remember I met a school vice principal who told me he does not want to be rich. He painted a very bad picture of rich people in the society that he just had to say he never pray to be rich. We are in a society full of pretence. Even when you deny the fact that you like money, you cannot deny the fact that you like those things that money can buy.

Money does not solve all human problems, but it has a role to play in all human affairs. The truth is that as long as we are here on earth, we all need money and the more of it you have the better. Because the more money you have to spend the more freedom you have to decide what you want to be. You can easily decide to be religious or generous. To pretend not to desire plenty of money is deception and pride in manifestation. The desire to be rich is natural not optional. To be otherwise is abnormal. In fact, the desire to get money is usually unending, because human wants are insatiable.

The only simple truth we all need to appreciate is this: members of the society must consciously learn about money in order to have a better-developed society. The laws of money must not be applied in isolation; other values of importance must be well understood and applied. The values of love, humility, respect for other people's lives and rights, faithfulness and sincerity and the likes are very important. However, this book is not meant for any of them. None of the values should be denied or ignored. Even in a society where majority pretend not to like money, many frauds and crimes in the society are traceable to desire to make money or lack of money.

The first step towards building success in business is the readiness to assert that money is a major motivation in business. It is the ability to declare boldly how much you need money and how much getting it means to you that set you on the path of business success. A lot of people are not ready to be called greedy. What people call greed is in all of us at different levels? It is a natural thing. Never give in to intimidation out of pretence.

Money is necessary, you need it and you are looking for it. For now, money is very important until the world will find replacement for money. Even when the world finds replacement for money, the value that money carries will still be very important. Because whatever it is that replaces money will carry the same value that money carries and do the same thing that money does. It was like that even in the era of trade by barter.

A man analyzed the Nigerian society and said: Hausa man controls politics, Yoruba man lead in academics while the Igbo man controls the commerce or business. If that is true, I know one reason why the Igbo man must lead in the business world. An Igbo man acknowledges the importance of money in all he does. No pretence about it. He consciously plans his way to make money. Attach appropriate respect and value to money and money will identify with you in a matter of time.

1. HOW TO MAKE MONEY

What then is money? Money is the medium of exchange. The first principle in the law of money is that something must be exchanged for money. If I need more money, I just think of what I can give people to get money from them. For people to part with their money, you must give what they appreciate; something that meets their needs or solve their problem. They also need to feel that what they are getting in return is of more value than the money they are giving you. How does that happen?

By law of substance and by law of design! You must look for something of accurate substance; something that is actually worth it. That is the **law of substance.** It is all about what value your offer provides, the problem it solves and the substitute it provides. Your offer could be a product or a service. What matters is the value not the name. That is why I don't need an office before I start business. When I started, my office was anywhere I was. I later got an office, but that was after I had made some money.

You must also have to design your product or service in a way that people will appreciate to the extent of being ready to part with their money for it. This is the **law of design**. It is not all about what it is; it is about what people think it is. Corporate organizations all over the world spend millions to ensure that their products meet peoples taste. It is one of the secrets of business success.

The principle of making money is the same, both in business and in employment. Your employer did not employ you because he likes your face or your name. Companies do not employ because of certificates. They employ because of what you can offer, because of your service. You may ask, why do employers require certificates before employing people?

The reason is simple. They believe that certificate is a good pointer to what you can offer, since what one can do is not naturally written in the face. If your service does not conform to the testimony of your certificate on the long run, they must necessarily show you the way out. Your employer employs you just for the money you can make for him and nothing more.

Let me quickly say this, that if your employer agrees to pay you fifty thousand naira a month, he must be sure you can make one hundred and fifty thousand naira a month for him. I tell you, if you are in your private business you will make multiples of that a month, it is only a matter of time.

What is the lesson? Learn about making money. Read books on the subject of money, attend seminars and ask questions about money. You are on your way to financial freedom; it is just a matter of time. This attitude will help you keep your job for the mean time, and will place you on the path of success in your private business. Give value and value will come back to you. It will come both in terms of money and other good things of life.

SEE THE GOLD MINE
Devise something of value that you can give people for their money in that place where you find yourself. That is all you need. They will pay you good money in return. What if they are poor people? What if they don't have money? You may want to ask.

Know this one thing. Everybody has problems, rich or poor. This is because definition of problem varies per person, per time and per circumstances. In addition, we are all facing the challenge of coping with our environment. The more we understand our world's environment, the more mastery we gain in life. Know also that everybody is looking for solution to his problems. Another thing you have to know is that everybody has money. The difference is only in the amount of money you have and how you spend it. Poor people are not always people who have no money. They are people who don't know how to spend the little they have. They don't know how to use the money they have to generate more money for themselves. They don't know how to use small money to finance big ideas and reproduce the money in thousand times.

IT IS EASIER TO GET MONEY FROM THE POOR
The point here is that, the fact that you find yourself in a community that appears poor does not say you cannot make

money there. It is even easier to get money from poor people than from the rich. Have you not observed that most rich men think very well before they part with their money?

First, because money is a security to the one that possesses it. The rich man does not want to lose this security. He does not want to become like the poor man and so he thinks very well before he parts with a penny. This is just because he does not want to leave his comfort zone.

Secondly, every rich man, especially if he has generated his riches through wise saving, strategic decision making and hard work, understands the principle of wealth creation. It is: **"be fast to make money, be slow to spend it"**.

The third reason is that the rich do not spend in penny, they spend in big amounts. Whether he is spending on himself or on other people, at least a relatively big amount would be involved. The people around the rich men do not normally ask them for small money, they ask for something that is as big as the status of the rich man.

Imagine that you are the direct younger brother of Alhaji Aliko Dangote and you are an undergraduate of the University of Ibadan. If you are returning to campus for the new session, will you ask him for N4,000 (Four Thousand Naira Only) as transport back to school, when you can go on the best flight? Will you ask him to give you money to secure an accommodation off campus in a house without a toilet?

Naturally, you will never ask for those ridiculous things. You will ask for big money that the man would need to write you a cheque. In fact, you will ask for an amount that you would need to open a bank account into which your rich brother can instruct his bankers to transfer money for your school expenses. You know what? The bigger the amount involved, the more thoughtful the giver becomes before he gives out the money. You will learn more of this principle in the subsequent chapters. The point I am making here is that anywhere you find yourself, there are boundless opportunities there to make as much money as you wish.

There are opportunities to make money from the poor and the middle class, especially when it becomes a game of numbers. There are opportunities to make money from the rich, particularly when volume and a big amount is involved.

ENJOY THE LARGE NUMBER
Many of us would not naturally find ourselves among the rich people. And of course, how many people are rich in the whole country? Less than one percent of the population is in the rich class. And so, if you are focusing your attention on what you can only collect from the rich, you might be disappointed. The rich only give to their fellow rich men. Until when you get to their level, know your level. If you are a poor bricklayer, and you are looking for a rich man to give you building contracts, you may end up disappointed.

A rich man can only give his building contract to a fellow rich contractor who will engage the poor people to do the work and give them peanuts, while he smiles to the bank with the huge profit. For the rich man to give big contract to a poor man is a miracle. And miracles don't happen every-day. The world does not operate on miracles, it operates on principles. Principles work all the times. One principle of life is: "know your level and take advantage of it". If you apply the principle consistently, you will soon join the rich class, and then the rich will freely give you their huge money. The poor people who want to start collecting from the rich by all means, over night, they are those dreaded armed robbers on the high ways.

The good news is that you can collect all you need from the poor people. Why? Because they are in the majority; they have the number. It is like that in any society including nations like the United State of America, Britain, France, and China. It is from this poor populace that you can get all you want. And the wisdom you apply to what you get from them is what translates you from the colony of the poor people to the class of the rich personalities.

Another reason why you will get all you want from the poor people apart from their large population is that it is easier for poor people to part with their money. This is partly because their spending usually involves small amount of money at a time. But they can repeat that small spending a thousand times without thinking about it. Any poor man that thinks very well before spending his small money will soon leave the company of the poor to join the class of the rich. Any rich man that is a free spender, who does not think before spending, big or small, is rich by mistake and will soon come back to join his fellow poor class. This is neither a curse nor a prayer; it is a principle of life. Any society or system where this principle does not apply is in economic danger.

One other thing you need to know about why it is easier to get more money from the poor is this: the poor spend much of their income on consumption and on consumables. And consumption is a compulsory exercise in life. Whether you are rich or poor, you still have to consume. You have to eat food, wear clothes, wear shoes and live under a shelter. Nobody can exist without those things. Even somebody who does not make any income must still eat and put on something as clothes to cover his body. And because the poor are always under serious pressure to meet these needs, they think less when making spending decisions. They don't usually have time to plan their expenses.

Now, take this example. If you are selling something that goes for N50 (fifty naira) per item, you only need to sell one hundred pieces to make N5000 (Five thousand Naira). Selling essential, consumable items you can conveniently sell hundred pieces a day or at most within three days. Look at a neighbor selling costly articles that are only meant for the rich class, he may take up to six days to sell only one article of N5000(five thousand naira). Within those six days, you have sold two hundred pieces of your small products with a turnover of about N10.000 (Ten thousand Naira) while your neighbor is still struggling to sell one unit of his "for the rich only" product.

Not only that. You may discover that it is possible for you to make a profit of about N5 (five naira) per unit of your own product while it would be very difficult for that neighbor to make up to N500 (five hundred naira) per unit of his article. You may be surprised to know that it is more profitable to be a bread seller than being a motor dealer. This is with particular reference to what is called return on investment in the business world. How many people buy cars in a year? Very few people do. How many people buy bread in a day? Millions of people do. If you go to the yard of a motor dealer, you will see cars that have been there for years, nobody to buy them. And they don't usually appreciate in value. They depreciate in value quickly, because they go with fashion.

At the advent of GSM Communication in Nigeria, I took part in the business. I started with distribution of recharge cards and vouchers and later to sale of GSM handsets. I soon discovered that it is much more profitable selling cards and vouchers than selling handsets. Cards are fast moving and less fashion driven while handsets are slow moving and highly fashion driven. And so, I quickly adjusted and concentrated on selling cards and vouchers. You ask whether I am still in card business today? No. I have found a better alternative and I have to go for it.

Why all this explanation, you may want to ask? It is for you not to misplace your priority. Stop looking up. Look down, you will find all the riches you desire. Never over look the rural populace. You can get more money than you ever thought possible from them.

One other reason why you will get money easily from the poor is this: when you are dealing with the poor, you face less competition. They are not as selective as the rich class; their tastes are not as high as that of the rich people. And so you have enough opportunity to learn by mistakes among the local populace. They don't criticize that much. They go for what is available without much complaint. In fact they sympathize with you most times.

Therefore, enjoy all the opportunities where you are and make money as much as you desire.

JOIN THE MARKETERS

There are many ways you can define marketing. I may not be able to go into various definitions since definition or even theory of marketing is not our objective here. All you need to know is that in Marketing, you find consumers for your products or services. You don't only find customers but consumers, loyalists or those you may call faithfuls or supporters. Here, you strategically get your idea to the targeted audience. Any idea, service or product that does not sell is worthless, as far as the business world is concerned. Therefore, you need to master the art of marketing. Do you need to get a degree in marketing in order to be able to make the money you desire? Absolutely 'No'. Do you need to learn the art of marketing? Capital 'Yes'. Just like I categorically assure you of the possibility of making as much as you want, I can also categorically state that your ability to market yourself, your ideas or products is the key.

In developed economies like that of the United States of America, marketing is becoming the most lucrative exercise. There was a time Engineering was the most lucrative thing. At another time, it was Accounting and Finance. At another time, it turned to Agriculture and then to Information and Communication Technology. While certain other fields of human endeavor or profession normally obey the law of diminishing returns in terms of economic future and relevance, there are others with unlimited potentials. These professions would rather become universal affairs with time but they would never lose their relevance. You ask what I mean by becoming universal affairs? It becomes basic or prerequisite, which everybody must possess. Years ago, ability to speak English language was a very profitable skill in the Nigerian society. Those were the days of colonial masters. At least you can work as an interpreter for the white men or work as secretary or typist.

Today, speaking English language is universal in the Nigerian society. Even the illiterates speak English; at least they have their own version, which they communicate with. Nobody looks for an interpreter anymore. Ability to type with manual typewriter was a sellable skill some years ago. You see people establishing typing pools, having many apprentices. It later turned to electric typewriters and later to the use of computer typesetting. But today, the story is different. Most executives can type on their own with their laptops or even desk top computers. Nobody looks for typist to employ anymore. In fact, most organized companies have monetized the services of typists or secretaries for their managers. Today, typing or ability to do some secretarial work is now a universal affair. That is why you see all advertisement for employment usually request potential employees to have skill in the use of computer. Even if you are to be employed as production manager or trainee, you must be able to use computer. You remember that driving was enough skill to put someone on government or company payroll a few years back. Now, services of drivers are being monetized. It is now a universal thing, almost every adult can drive.

What is the point here? Marketing is essential to money making in today's society and you must know how to do it. If you are the type who hates marketing, you need to change your orientation or you limit your potentials in today's world. Even looking for job is marketing; it is marketing your skills. Without a little bit of marketing, you may find it difficult to get a job of your dream.

I am not talking of marketing stuff as we learnt in our various academic campuses. After all, there are people who have degrees in marketing and still cannot market themselves talk less of marketing any product or service. I am not in any way condemning the theories of marketing as we learnt in school.

The lecturers and teachers of marketing in our institutions are doing wonderful job. Some people must take custody of the theories and the fundamentals. They are the custodians of the theories and traditions of marketing and we learn a lot from them. The truth is that marketing is more than a course of study; it is an art which you must learn. It is a culture which you must build and it is a habit which you must develop. You may not be a specialist or a professional marketer. But you must know and practice the art of marketing as a generalist. That is a major key to making money in today's society.

2. HOW TO SAVE MONEY
In accounting, saving money means making money, because, when you reduce your cost you indirectly increase your profit.

There are people who make plenty of money but never achieve anything tangible with it. The problem, most of the time, is that they know how to make money, but they never learn how to save money. If you are making money and you don't have savings, you are not in any way better than somebody that is not making money. You are both prone to financial embarrassment.

Both the one who does not know how to make money and the one who does not save will never be able to take advantage of opportunity. When opportunity comes, it asks for your preparation and saving is one good way of preparing for the day of opportunity. In fact, many of the people complaining of lack of capital to start business are people who lack discipline to save from the little that comes to them. There is no level of income that is too small for you not be able to save out of it.

ECONOMICS OF SAVING
Remember what we learnt in our secondary school economics about the motives of saving money? That lesson will be very useful here.

WHY YOU NEED TO SAVE MONEY
1. For transactions: You save money for your day-to-day transactions. You save to ensure that you keep buying the consumables in the days ahead even when your income flow is not on daily basis. Here, we talk of daily needs of feeding, clothing, transport and other regular maintenance for you and your family. If you have not learnt how to save, you will always have crisis in this area.

2. For Precaution: You save for the purpose of taking care of unforeseen circumstances, like sickness, accident, theft, lost of job and so on. You don't pray for these, but they do happen. In case they happen, what is your plan? In case you lose your job today, what is your plan? You say God forbid? God forbid alone is not enough. You need to do something.

3. For Speculation: This implies the money you save to take advantage of possible business opportunities that may come your way. You must master the art of saving in such a way that you clearly demarcate your savings into these categories.

You must also have the discipline to maintain the boundary. Avoid using money meant for precaution on transactions. Avoid using the one made for speculation on precaution and transactions. The secret of the very rich people is that they are committed to saving for speculation. Money saved for speculation is the real saving. This is what is used to take advantage of business opportunities. Be careful with people around you who will never save from the little they have, but will rather want to transfer their transaction, precaution and speculation burdens to you.

The practice of saving must be part of you, otherwise you will never get out of the rat race, financial struggle. That your income is small is not an excuse. If you are earning one thousand naira and you cannot save out of it, the day you earn one hundred thousand naira you will never be able to save a kobo.

Everybody can save, even those who are being fed by someone. Everybody has income, even a street beggar has income. The people that are working, their income is called earned income. The people that are sustained by other people, their income is called unearned income. The fact remains that everybody has income and so everybody can save.

Students can save. I discussed some years ago with a woman who told me how she saved from her pocket money in her university days. Out of the savings she bought a refrigerator with which she started selling fish and food ingredients in the hostel. When she graduated after two years, she had a savings of up to two hundred thousand naira. That was in the year 2004.

One major cause of poverty in Nigeria is the poor attitude of the people to saving. That is why banks have to engage in elaborate promotions before people will bring their money to the bank. Apart from what is the face value of the money you saved, ability to save is a demonstration of discipline and financial intelligence.

SAVING MORE THAN CASH
There are various ways you can save apart from cash saving, and it may be a wiser step to save in those other forms.

CONSIDER STOCKS AND SHARES
Even a student can raise as low as four thousand five hundred naira to buy from an initial public offer-IPO of a newly listed company. Most of the time you buy with the money you can afford to lose. Do that as many times as possible over the years.

I was discussing with somebody recently. The man had shares in one of the old generation banks in Nigeria, which he bought years back. He has actually forgotten that he bought so many shares in that bank because it has appreciated over the years together with various right and bonus issues which he had bought all along. When we converted the shares to the current market value, it was worth about five million naira.

You know what? He can choose to dispose the shares for business purposes. He can use the certificate as collateral to collect loan from a bank or any other lender while his investment in shares still continues to appreciate. Yet, this is an investment he had even forgotten about. It simply means if he did not buy the shares at the time he did, he could as well have wasted the money on things of no consequence. Because of the recent slide in the capital market, many Nigerians avoid the stock market like a plague. Many people want fast money. However, for the ones who would be patient, stock market still remains a good place to save your money.

CONSIDER INSURANCE POLICY
Insurance is one area that most Nigerians neglect simply because of ignorance. They complain it is difficult to make claims from insurance companies in the event the risk insured comes true. Whatever you say about it, Insurance policy, especially life policy, is still one of the easiest ways to save.

I was discussing with a man few years ago who told me how his employers compelled all workers to take life insurance policy. The premium is deducted from workers salaries up front. In less than three years, a junior worker like him had got up to two hundred thousand naira savings in the policy. That was far back in 2006. The policy allows him to borrow up to 95% of his total contribution at the lowest interest rate you can get anywhere. Instead of being biased, you better find out. It works.

CONSIDER PENSION SCHEME, HEALTH TRUST SCHEME AND THRIFT SCHEMES

Go for schemes like pension, health insurance or thrift, especially if you are a salary earner or a low income earner. It pays to save without return or interest than not saving at all. These schemes are everywhere. Ask your employer. Ask an insurance man. Walk into a bank and make enquiry.

3. HOW TO SPEND MONEY

This is the third of the three most important lessons you must learn about money before you can make your way to riches. You may be making millions of dollars per annum, but without proper spending habit you are ending nowhere. What matters is not how much you earn, but how well you spend it.

SPENDING TO MAKE MONEY

Each time you spend, always think of how your spending can bring money back to you. Avoid spending when you know the money once spent would be gone forever. Give priority to spending that will bring more money back to you, now or in future. Be an investor rather than a mere spender.

INVESTOR SPENDING VS WASTER SPENDING HABITS

You remember the concept of national income in macroeconomics as we learnt in the school? If you did not do it in school or you have forgotten, there is no problem, you can still get the principle.

$$Y=C+S+I$$
Where:
Y=Income
C=Consumption
S=Savings
I=Investment

If you adopt the principle of this formula, you will never have idle fund. It is either you consume or you save or you invest. Or better still, you do the three at the same time. The priority you give to each depends on you and your life goals.

Consumption is compulsory but controllable. Savings and investments are voluntary but most essential. We all spend, but in spending, some are wasters while others are investors. It is all a matter of habit. The man who consumes at the expense of saving and investing is a waster, because he spends his money on his wants and not on his needs. Your wants are things that are good but you can still do well without them. Your needs are those that matter to your existence and you have ways of meeting them. Your needs depends on your level and your goal. Of a truth, everybody wants to buy all that money can buy. And everybody has the right to buy all that money can buy, as long as you can afford it.

PRIORITY CONSUMPTION

You are not doing yourself any good by trying to avoid necessary consumptions. You must eat good food, the best food at your level. Put on decent cloth at your level. One thing is, whatever your level is, you should live in good accommodation. The accommodation where I live today is good for me at my level. Obviously, in the next three years my level must have grown above this.

All these have their ways of reflecting on your life's achievement. They all have effects on your investment and business life. If you don't eat well your health is in danger. Without good health you cannot reason well nor create ideas and you cannot perform optimally on your duty. If you don't eat well and you think you are performing well, try to eat well and then measure and compare your performance. You will see a clear difference. The same goes for living in decent accommodation. Eating is investing; it is investing on your health. It only must be at your level and must be thoughtfully controlled. Always maintain a balance.

Good food does not have to be costly. Decent accommodation does not have to be expensive. Unfortunately we are in a society where many believe buying at exorbitant prices is a sign of affluence. Some believe eating all manner of junks is a sign of being a big man. I remember that some years back, our community people believed that diabetics and potbelly are sicknesses of rich people. Funny enough, many of the so called rich people were not actually rich. They were simply pretending, living to please the society at the expense of their lives.

COMMITMENT TO SAVING

It is easier to consume more than to save. People don't need much persuasion for them to eat or consume. It is even very easy to consume above your income. Savings, however takes commitment.

What is saving? It is reducing your consumption today so you can increase it tomorrow. Some of my associates sometimes accuse me of being stingy. Just because I don't visit fast food joints as often they expect. Fast food houses are doing good business, but you must know whether it is ripe for you to buy a plate of food for two thousand five hundred naira or look for a cheaper but good alternative. Sit down and calculate how much you are spending on phone calls, most of which are avoidable. You will be surprised at the amount of money. The man who drinks a bottle of beer for three hundred and fifty naira a day can save a lot of money in a year if he stops or reduces the consumption. I remember the story of a commissioner in one of the states in Nigeria who spent three hundred and fifty thousand naira on GSM calls in a month! That was far back around 2003.

KNOW YOUR ASSETS AND LIABILITIES

Very many people have worked for years without acquiring any asset. The problem is not that their income is too small to do so, but it is because they don't know what an asset is. Most of what people call properties are mere liabilities.

When I bought my first car some years ago, a lot of people rejoiced with me, some even appeared happier than myself. The truth is that I was seeing what many of my well-wishers were not seeing. Most of the times, we are supposed to sympathize with car owners more than we rejoice with them, because a car is to many of these owners, more of a liability than an asset. When it collects from you more than it gives you or it has no way of bringing back to you the money you used to buy it, then it is a liability. When it is more of consumption than investment in nature, it is a liability not an asset. When it has no way of helping you to save part of your regular income or when it is all about cost and not returns or income, it is a liability not an asset.

In a country where the cost of fuel is very high, somebody must think twice before putting his money on a car. Think about using a personal car now, how much cost does it save you compared to the entire car running expenses. Think of fueling, regular maintenance and spare parts.

Many road accidents are as a result of the fact that many vehicle owners could not afford necessary maintenance of the vehicles they put on the road. And so, they take the risk of putting the vehicles on the road anyhow and endanger the lives of other road users. The issue is not only about car. I only used car as an example. Good accommodation is good, but you have to think the cost benefit way before you go for one.

WHEN YOUR LIABILITY BECOMES AN ASSET
If you learn to be thoughtful and time conscious, these things we call liabilities will serve the asset purpose in your hand. And that is what they are meant for. There is a man who makes up to a million naira or dollars from his home or office with just about 30 minutes conversation on phone with people that matter. To such a man, a GSM phone is an asset, not a liability. To people who have nothing profitable doing with telephone, possessing one is a liability; a luxury. Uncontrolled telephone expenses alone, if not properly controlled, can keep somebody at the lower level of life financially forever.

An executive who wins multimillion naira contracts must of a necessity go on a fine car and costly decent dresses. To him these are not luxuries, they are necessities, because it is by the way he dresses he would be addressed. To reach the level where luxury becomes an asset takes time and commitment, but it is attainable. Everybody can be there and that is why you are reading this book. I must also say this: it is not as if some are destined to be at that level while others are not. Financial freedom is what anyone can achieve by adequate planning, discipline, hard work and faith.

The lesson here is, identify things that are liability to you at every point in time and avoid them. **If you can't afford it, you can avoid it.** What is luxury to you today will certainly become a necessity tomorrow; it only takes time and the right attitude.

Instead of complaining about lack of money or capital, address these vital issues of your life. You will be surprised how much is already available to you that you can only harness with the right attitude or mind set. Get rid of pretence. Be realistic. Learn to be hard on yourself rather than being hard on the society or even the government. Take responsibility for your life. It pays on the long run.

BARGAINING HABIT CENTRAL TO RIGHT SPENDING

One thing that is common to poor people is their poor bargaining habit. They don't usually buy at the best price. When it comes to negotiation, they are easily intimidated. A poor person here does not necessarily mean somebody that has no money to eat. Whether they have money or not, one thing is that they don't control money; they don't control their own economy. Money controls them and economy controls them. Remember that poverty is a matter of the mind, likewise riches.

If you see somebody who goes to market and buys things at whatever price it is offered, watch him. There are two possibilities. It is either the person will end up a poor man or woman in a matter of time or the source of money he is parading to have is not genuine.

When you value money, money will come to you. Avoid paying more when you can pay less. An average person makes up to ten transactions a day, big or small, ranging from taking a taxi, to buying food items, buying clothing materials and so on. If you are able to save fifty naira per transaction, calculate how much you would save in a day, in a month and then in a whole year. Little drops of water make a mighty ocean. Besides, you are using these small transactions to learn a habit that will help you tremendously in big transactions that will come your way in future.

Don't be ashamed to bargain, never allow the other party to intimidate you. Avoid anything not negotiable, except where there is no alternative to it. Don't buy where they use price tag when you can get the same quality in a place where you will negotiate and save some cost. Don't allow the pride that goes with supermarket buying to control you. Anywhere you can get what you want is market. No one is super. Avoid impulse buying, that is purchase without thinking.

Always ensure you collect your balance, no matter how small it is. Carry enough lower denominations of your currency. That is the reason why the Central Bank of Nigeria sometime ago reintroduced lower denominations of naira and kobo. Unfortunately, many people, even the poor individuals are ashamed to carry coins.

KEEP YOUR MONEY NEAT
Keeping your money neat and well arranged will normally make you a wise spender. People generally value money when it is new and neat than when it is dirty. Ironically, both the neat money and the dirty ones carry the same value, but one attracts

more respect than the other. You can tell the one that is more respected and better appreciated.

DEVELOP THE SALARY MENTALITY
I have come to hate working for salary, particularly when one has to depend solely on salary. It is only good as a last resort.

However, there is an advantage of salary work. The advantage is in the mentality of the salary earners. Salary places a limitation on them and they usually learn to live within that limitation. They plan within their income no matter how small. That planning mentality makes salary work attractive. An average roadside mechanic makes more money in a month than a school principal. But by all standards, the principal lives a more decent life than the mechanic. The difference is in the mentality each of them carries.

The mechanic spends today's income freely expecting another one will come tomorrow. Any day his expectation is not met, he goes borrowing. The principal always plan his expenses within his income, even if he owes, he hardly owes above what his next month salary can carry. At the end of the day, the salary earner is better off.

BE AN INDIAN GIVER
Indians are known to be good managers. They manage business to success anywhere under any condition. An Indian does not give out anything without expecting something in particular in return. Your giving must be guided by that

principle. Prioritize your giving based on what each can bring back to you in cash or in kind, physically or spiritually.

And that is why salary work is deceptively attractive to many people. Because the salary earners look decent, you hardly think they have financial problem. Until you have tried a successful business of your own, you will not know that most salary jobs are like self-imprisonment. What the mechanic needs is not a change of job; it is a change of habit and he will be in a better position to employ his school principal friend. Anybody starting his own business needs that type of mentality, salary mentality. He cannot afford to be a free spender. Most successful business people are those who place themselves on salaries, even though they own the entire business.

APPLY APPROPRIATION STRATEGY
There is something big organizations do, they don't declare dividends from profit; they declare dividends from appropriation. It simply means they don't regard all their profit as income to share. They first save for the future before spending in the present. Whatever your source of income is, always save before you spend. It is advisable that your entire income goes to the bank first, then from there withdraw a determined amount for spending after you have directed the one that is meant for saving. It is not always easy, but it is worth it. Nothing good comes easy. If you are an employee, always insist that your salary be paid through the bank. The advantages cannot be compared with the small amount the

bank will charge you for their services.

PAY YOURSELF FIRST
If you are in business, determine an appropriate salary for yourself. Otherwise you will end up spending above your income. The salary you will pay yourself must be realistic in the light of the income from the business and your own needs. In other words, it must not be too small that will make you starve and it must not be too big to make you extravagant to endanger your savings and the future of your business

SALARY FROM SALARY
As a salary earner the best way to secure your future financially is to pay yourself salary from what your employer pays you. That is, you don't regard all that your employer pays you as disposable income. Determine an amount from it that you will pay yourself and send the rest to your savings or your investment account. Be disciplined to follow it. If the standard you have set is too difficult for you to follow, adjust the proportion but never change the principle.

READINESS TO OWE
Anybody that is afraid of owing can hardly have plenty of money. Be ready to owe but owe carefully. Owe responsibly. Improve your capacity to owe by developing your ability to manage resources and improving your personality. Capacity to owe depends on trust and confidence. Nobody wants to lend his money to somebody he does not trust or have confidence in. In business, it is not only a matter of what you

are but also of what people think and feel about you.

Owing for productive purposes is one of the best ways you can attain growth and prosperity in the business world. Owing for productive reasons is called leveraging.

CONSISTENCY AND INVESTMENT

7

To be a success in business, you must be able to master something, something in particular, by experience. To master a trade or industry takes time. It takes consistency. **Even an imbecile when he has done something consistently for so long enough time is going to become a champion in that thing.** Don't become a jack of all trade and master of none. Rather, spend enough time in selecting and studying what you are going to do before you start at all.

As much as I do not support being dogmatic or fanatical, I advise people to stay long enough doing what they are doing and where they are. Every business has its own season of fortune, because economy moves in a cycle. When the cycle comes to a particular business or sector, it is the people that have stayed long enough to have mastered the business that will benefit from the fortune. If you are not making the desired progress in a particular business, investigate the reasons for your failure instead of running to another one that you think is lucrative.

If you go to another business that you don't know about, before you get settled in that one the tide might have gone down. Possibly the fortune of your former business has come by that time and it may not be easy to carry your investment back to that place.

LOOK BEFORE YOU LEAP
Each time you want to start a new business, do enough investigation about it first to avoid waste and rushing back. Every business that brings money has risks, because returns and risks go together

Ask questions about the risks before you get excited about the promised returns. You ask questions about risks not necessarily because you want to avoid them, but to prepare yourself for them and how to reduce them or reduce their effects when they come. Never plan to avoid risks, because avoiding risks is avoiding returns/profit. Of course, there are risks that are avoidable. Such you should reasonably avoid or prevent. Business is about taking calculated risks.

The preparation against risks will both save you from some business embarrassments and give you the needed staying power in times of trouble. However, you must be positive and do your investigation with a possibility mind-set

POWER OF INVESTMENT
There is no other legitimate way to abundance and wealth than unbroken habit of investment. There is no other guaranteed way to bumper harvest except the habit of sowing. This requires the ability to see into the future.

I listened to an interview granted by Former President Olusegun Obasanjo recently. Among other questions, the interviewer requested to know about the history of Obasanjo Farms, particularly the Otta Farm. He responded by saying that he acquired his first farm land in 1967 as part of his preparation for retirement from the Nigerian Army. Since then he made it an habit to acquire farm lands anywhere available as he was able to raise money. The Otta farm land was one of those acquired after the one of 1967. Obasanjo would later become the Nigerian Head of States about 8years after and retired from the Army 12years after.

I bet it, if you used 12 years to consistently plan for retirement, retirement can never be a burden to you. It does not matter the size of your salary or at what grade level you retired. It takes a man of vision to consistently prepare himself for retirement over twelve years. And to even think of farming of all things as far back as 1967 takes

vision and commitment.

You must learn to invest from what you have, no matter how small. Invest money. Invest time. Invest energy and any other thing you have.

INVESTORS VS TRADER MENTALITIES

An investor starts his business from the heart, while the trader starts from the hand. That is why money is the most important factor to a trader. An investor takes risks that a trader will want to avoid. Why? He has developed his capacity to take risks over time. Also, because what he is putting in business is not only money. Dr. Michael Leboeuf puts it this way: "**success is a result of making good decisions, and good decision comes from good judgment. Good judgment comes from experience and experience comes from bad judgment**". This describes an investor. Bad judgments mean mistakes, which are not sometimes totally avoidable. To an investor, every mistake or setback carries the seeds of future success and he is smart enough to learn from them.

An investor sees opportunities where a trader sees adversities. To an investor, the business is owned by stakeholders. To a trader, the business is his personal property. An investor considers all stakeholders - shareholders, employees, customers, government, creditors and others as critical to business decisions. To a trader, the factor will either be himself or the money he intends to make.

CONSISTENCY AND INVESTMENT

Ultimately, the investor lasts and survives many tides while the trader goes down with the tides. The investor looks beyond just prosperity; he looks and plans for posterity. He thinks beyond just business success, he thinks about succession. To him money making cannot completely describe business success without consideration to other non quantitative values. Why many businesses that appear to be doing well die within a matter of few years is, most times, that people behind those businesses have trader mentalities.

So, behave like an investor and avoid the mistakes of a trader. Don't only evaluate a business or industry from what it brings today. Sow into the future. If you have tried and have not succeeded, try more but with knowledge. Don't spend all your profit; reinvest part or all of it for better return in the future. Whether you are an investor or a trader has nothing to do with the nature of business you engage in. It has nothing to do with whether you are in retail, wholesale, production, manufacturing or marketing business. It has nothing to do with whether you sell tangible products or intangible services. It has to do with your mentality, your values and your perspectives to business. It has to do with your fundamental views, motives and expectations from the business.

In the business world there are two sets of people, based on their mentalities - the traders and the investors. The traders think of today while the investors think of tomorrow. The traders look for money while the investors look for what money can buy for them. With or without money, the investor can start with whatever he has. You can invest your time, talents, energy and knowledge, even while you are still looking for money. The investors control the economy, while the economy controls the traders, all because the investors think of the future and buy the future.

The difference between a trader and an investor is their mindsets - their mentalities. And so whether one is a manufacturer and another is a distributor is not the issue here. Not everybody who is into manufacturing is an investor. As far as this analysis is concerned, not everyone who does retail business is a trader. There are thousands of manufacturing businesses that do not last for two years. There are purely trading businesses that have survived for decades. It is all about the mindset behind each business endeavor.

TALENTS, CHOICE AND ACTION POWER OF TALENTS

One thing we must all know is the importance of our gifts and talents to what each person would become in life. A man that ignores his gifts is a waster, because your highest resource is your talent. **'A man's gift will make way for him'**, so says the Bible. The business you will select must be the one that goes in line with your gift. It must be the one that will naturally help you to express your gift and talent. Therefore, the business is going to be fun to you rather than a hard task.

Teaching and disseminating problem solving information is just natural to me. That is why I choose what I am doing now. I can craft problem solving ideas. I can inspire people. When I do such things, I forget about food. Sometimes, even when I am slightly indisposed, the indisposition naturally disappears when I have an opportunity to inspire others with an idea I strongly believe in.

We all have strengths and weaknesses. Ability to identify your strength and build around it is central to business success. You do this as you improve on your weaknesses

POWER OF CHOICE
Life is what you make out of it. Poverty is a choice and wealth is a choice. In this case, there is nothing like luck. You don't become rich by chance. If you became rich by chance you cannot maintain the riches by chance. And you cannot be said to be rich until you are able to retain what you have. So, it is all a matter of choice. It is better you try and fail than not trying at all, because failure is not failure as long as you can learn from it and move on to do better. Act now.

THE ENTREPRENEUR, THE MINDSET AND ORIENTATION

8

THE ENTREPRENEUR

You must have heard the word "**entrepreneur**" as many times as possible, depending on your background. Entrepreneur or entrepreneurship is an all important word in this generation. I refer to this generation because the word entrepreneur has not always been in human history, even though the art of entrepreneurship has always being part of human existence.

The word entrepreneur was coined from a French origin by a French Economist J.B. Say around 1800. He said "**the entrepreneur shifts economic resources out of an area of**

lower productivity into an area of higher productivity and yield". J.B. Say's definition presupposed that resources will always be available, at least in the quantity that the real entrepreneurs can perceive them, even when the generality of people cannot. It further suggested that by nature, the resources are not always in the areas of the highest productivity and yield. There is a natural imbalance which creates huge opportunities for the entrepreneurs to add value to our world.

ART OF ENTREPRENEURSHIP
The art of entrepreneurship has always been part of human existence. There are many theories about evolution, creation and human development. The fact, however remains that if you take human history from any of these sources, you will clearly see the art of entrepreneurship. Another thing that will become clear as you review human history based on any of these traditions, is that wealth, riches, abundance and leadership have always been linked to entrepreneurial abilities of individuals and societies.

It was during one of my Pastor's teachings he mentioned that Abraham who is regarded as the Father of Faith both from Christian and Islamic traditions, was actually an entrepreneur. I was shocked to discover that the Bible actually portrayed Abraham as a farmer than as a priest in the temple of worship.

World history and religious sources established the fact that different groups of people and nations have taken political leadership of the entire world at different times in human history. At a time it was Egypt, at another time it was the Romans and so on. One thing that is clear in all the historical traditions is the fact that political leadership has always reside where economic power resides. Even when a kingdom has been elevated as a result of military conquests, it still requires economic power to establish itself and earn desired respect from other kingdoms. Economic power has also usually been a direct result of the entrepreneurial ability of a people. Entrepreneurial ability could be in production, development, art or trading and commerce.

In today's world the order is still the same. The world today is divided into the "developed" and "developing" countries. The real difference has always been in the entrepreneurial orientation and ability of the people of each country. It has always been about the deliberate efforts of the governments and the people of each country to encourage and develop entrepreneurial activities and orientation within the country.

So far, from the introductory page of this book up till this moment, the author's efforts have been directed towards promoting the importance of entrepreneurial ability and entrepreneurial thinking. It is critical to point out that most of the people who complain of lack of capital actually lack the entrepreneurial abilities which are the core that attract money and other resources.

ENTREPRENEURSHIP DEVELOPMENT PROGRAMME - THE ACADEMIC EFFORTS

I remember there was a particular course in my final year in the Polytechnic called "Entrepreneurial Development Program"-EDP. It was a very important course. That means of course, you cannot graduate with Higher National Diploma in Accountancy or any other business related courses without passing the EDP. Another way you know the importance of a course is by the "unit point" attached to it. EDP was a 4-four unit course. By implications if you have low grade in EDP, your overall grade at the end of the day will be low. The Unit Point is an indication of the weight the score from the course will carry on your Grade Point Average. The all important course EDP was taught by a Ph.D holder. Of course, at that time we had several other important courses that were handled by lecturers with lower academic and professional qualifications.

My explanations here point to the level of importance attached to the knowledge of entrepreneurship by the drafters of our curricula. Policy makers all over the world have in the recent past acknowledged the importance of entrepreneurship. Governments make deliberate efforts to emphasize the importance of entrepreneurship. The irony however, particularly in the developing countries is that the more of academic education people get, the less entrepreneurial abilities and orientation they seem to possess.

Our EDP classes used to be two times a week, two hours each. I can still visualize how the Doctor will stand in front of the

THE ENTREPRENEUR, THE MINDSET AND ORIENTATION

class reading his EDP material before the class. He never bothered whether or not the students concentrated. He came to class always 30 minutes behind schedule and left the class at least 30minutes ahead of time. Some class members would usually be busy with different irrelevant discussions in different small groups within the class room as he continued to read out his lecture material.

The bottom line is that, we were never interested in whatever the Doctor had to say. He also was never interested in whether the students concentrated or not. We never took him serious and he never took us serious. I tried to memorize as much as I thought was necessary for me to pass the course. I did pass the course with a "B" grade like some of my class mates. I can tell you that I cannot remember any particular point learnt from the several hours of attending that class. This, I am sure is applicable to many of my class mates.

If you asked me what the problem was? I can tell you now. The problem with the students was the same with the lecturer. We never had interest. We did not believe in the entire programme. We never had any orientation that corroborated the importance of entrepreneurship. I can tell you that even the lecturer did not believe what he was teaching. We were all brought up to believe that our training in the school was to prepare us for an employment somewhere. Even when there were millions of people who graduated years before us and are still searching without end for employment, we still believe we are going to school for some individuals or governments to employ us afterwards.

WHO WILL WORK FOR WHO

When I published the first edition of this book, the title was very controversial but caught a lot of attention. I obtained a six month bank loan to finance the publishing. I did most of the sales myself, despite the fact that I was still holding a paid employment at that time. I actually repaid the loan in two months instead of six months. The title sold itself, particularly in the eastern part of Nigeria where you have a significant portion of the population who believed in self employment.

One of the major suppliers to the company where I worked as the Financial Controller at that time bought and read my book. The man, like many other customers and suppliers of the company always liked to engage me in discussions about business, economy and current affairs. That might account for the reason why this particular successful business man and our other suppliers gladly bought my first published book. The man came back a few days later to engage me on the contents of my book. He appreciated most of the contents of the book and confessed to me how he has practiced some of the principles taught in the book even without knowing. He encouraged me and expressed his believe that I was going to be very successful in life if I continued that way.

At the end of all the encouragements he expressed his deep concern. He said, "**if everybody would read your book, there is going to be a big problem**". I asked, What problem?

He said, "**if all would read and practice what you wrote in the book, who then will remain as employees? Who will work for who?**" He seemed to be saying employees should not be allowed to see my book, otherwise employers will find it difficult to get workers to work for them.

Certainly, some people must, at one time or the other be employed by some other people. There is nothing wrong in being an employee. Of course, employment has a way of teaching us some important lessons of life. Those lessons will be useful even as self-employed, employer or entrepreneur later in life. However, it was very necessary to address the issue of entrepreneurship and financial freedom as hard as possible. Otherwise, it will remain just like our EDP lecture and lecturer in the school.

WHO IS AN ENTREPRENEUR

We are in a society where the majority is not taught the art of entrepreneurship. We have an adult population that is not taught the most important thing for their lives. It is like trying to teach somebody in a week, something contrary to what he has been learning for over twenty to twenty-five years. It is a big task. And that is what this entire book is all about. It is about re-orientation. It is about mindset reconstruction. It is about mentality. It is about encouraging people to take risks they have been taught to avoid for the past twenty to twenty-five years or more. We are out to make people, who have planned their entire lives and future on employment and job security, to start thinking of being self employed and taking the risk of an employer.

As a summary of what have been taught so far, I will make some highlights about entrepreneurship.

In a study conducted by the United States Small Business Administration Department, a total of five characteristics of an entrepreneur were revealed as follows:

1. Drive to relentlessly pursue success in spite of having to work long hours and high stress facing endless problems along the way.

2. Mental acumen manifested in the entrepreneur's creativity, crucial thinking, analytical abilities and originality.

3. Aptitudes for human relations necessary to motivate employees, selling to customers, negotiate with suppliers and convince lenders.

4. Communication skills necessary to enforce effective bi-directional communication whereby ideas and visions are made clear and explicit.

5. Technical ability and strategic management skills to foresee long run and short run implications for critical business decisions; knowing one's strength and weakness as well as competitors

In conclusion, the study revealed one more vital characteristic: "success of small enterprise depends on originality of ideas and opportunism. Small entrepreneurs enhance flexibility and adaptability of economics because individuals move faster than large enterprises. They speed up commercialization process by turning new ideas into new products and services leading to economic dynamism".

The essence of the foregoing is to enable you to measure yourself on the scale of entrepreneurial ability as presented above. The good news is that all these attributes could be developed by anyone who is determined to do so. By reading books, attending seminars, listening to audio and video tapes and by interaction with the right people, all these could be developed.

TEN QUALITIES OF A SUCCESSFUL ENTREPRENEUR

Interestingly, most of the qualities required to be successful entrepreneurs are very important for success in all other human endeavors, including paid employment. The difference is only the application.

I want to briefly highlight the qualities required of a successful entrepreneur which are useful in other areas of life.

1. Initiative: an entrepreneur must be ingenious and resourceful. He must be alert to opportunities.

THE ENTREPRENEUR, THE MINDSET AND ORIENTATION

2. Risks- Taking: he must be ready to take risks. An entrepreneur is not unaware of the possibility of failure. He, however must not be overwhelmed by fear of failure. Readiness to face challenges is critical to any lasting success in any area of life.

3. Leadership Mindset: he must be able to inspire confidence and loyalty among other people, like employees and business associates. He must have positive outlook towards people, showing a friendly interest in a pleasant and polite manner. An entrepreneur must possess all desirable qualities of a leader in other to attract loyalty from other people that matter to his entrepreneurial interests.

4. Result Oriented: this is about having objective, the achievement of which is capable to driving him to hard work, persistence and determination. He always has a worthwhile objective or expected results behind his actions.

5. Readiness to take Responsibility: one major difference between successful people and failures in life is the willingness to take responsibility for their actions. The successful people are people who can take responsibility for their decisions, even when such decisions turn out to be wrong. The businessman must be willing and capable of assuming complete responsibility for the operation and success of his enterprise.

6. Organizing ability: the entrepreneur is at all times required to organize resources in a way to produce results. Resources here include human and non-human resources. However, organizing humans is the most critical responsibility of an entrepreneur.

7. Decisiveness: to be successful, an entrepreneur must be someone who can think quickly and accurately when decisions are required to be taken. This involves a level of risks taking which is hallmark of entrepreneurship.

8. Perseverance: even with the best of all plans, business outcome may not be as positive as planned. An entrepreneur must be somebody who can be persistent and enduring despite all odds.

9. Self Confidence: this has to do with confidence, independent mindedness, individuality and optimism.

10. Future Orientation: an entrepreneur's decisions are usually driven by the thought of the future than the thought of the present. He has foresight and future perspective on issues.

STRAIGHT TO POINTS

9

BUSINESSES YOU CAN START EVEN WITHOUT CAPITAL

*W*hat I will do here is to list out some businesses from where you can make your choice. You should also know that the list is inexhaustible.

You can also think of new ideas or modify the existing ones and make your money as you wish.

I will also explain how you can start or operate some of them. The most important things to consider in making selection will be made available for guidance at last.

BUSINESSES YOU CAN START EVEN WITHOUT CAPITAL

1. Marketing and supplying other people's product
2. Information brokerage
3. Catering, small chops and fast food services
4. Phone calls, recharge cards and GSM accessories
5. Parking space rentals
6. Interior decoration
7. Greeting cards production
8. Mailing list services
9. Website design
10. Poultry
11. Bakery and confectionaries
12. Car wash services
13. Fish farming
14. Computer Engineering, networking and sales
15. Recruitment agency
16. Paper and nylon recycling
17. Laundry services
18. Professional consultancy services
19. Management consultancy services
2. Party rentals
21. Health and fitness centre
22. Self Improvement seminars
23. Stocks and shares
24. Estate agency
25. Property and fund management
26. Book writing and publishing

27. Informational book reproduction and sales
28. Photo and video production and lamination
29. Production and marketing of fashionable hats
30. Ice block production
31. Daycare Centre for Children/ After School Service
32. Production of body cream
33. Commercial pig farming
34. Grass cutter production
35. Catfish production
36. Commercial sheep production
38. Commercial goat production
39. Rabbit farming
40. Snail farming
41. Production of edible mushrooms
42. Production of body lotion and jelly
43. Production of hair cream and hair oil
44. Production of detergents
45. Production of handbags
46. Production of fruit juice
47. Production of ice cream and yoghurt
48. Production of zobo drink and ginger drink
49. Production of custard powder
50. Information search service
51. Security service agency
52. Vegetable garden
53. Herbs and flower growing
54. Newspaper Clipping
55. Bumper Stickers

56. Bulletin Billboards
57. Radio and Television Productions
58. Research Publications
59. Travelling and Tour Agencies
60. Production of Plantain Chips
61. Documentary Clips Production etc.

BEGINNERS CAPACITY

Note that most of the businesses mentioned above are suitable for beginners. Why? None requires huge capital for you to start. Most of them do not ask for 24 hours a day from you. Only one person can start them. You would have made thousands or millions before you need payroll for extra hands. Most of them could be carried on in your home; you don't need office accommodation in the first place. That is why I have not talked about how to establish a flourmill or a petroleum refinery. It is not about how to obtain an oil-prospecting license from Ministry of Petroleum Resources.

Many of these businesses do not require a high level of education. You don't need to be located in Abuja or Lagos in order to do any of these businesses. They are applicable and available at any point in time and anywhere. They are carefully selected.

MARKETING OTHER PEOPLE'S PRODUCTS

Marketing other people's products is called different names all over the world. Some call it Dealership, others call it Networking, Brokerage, Agency, etc. Whatever name you want to call it, the bottom-line is, it is an uncommon way of generating income. Often times your income is tax free in a country like Nigeria. You supply, collecting your commission on sales, remit the balance to the source or producer. Terms vary from producer to producer.

At times you would be expected to make the advertisement yourself. In some cases, the owner of the product makes the advertisement, publicity and promotion. Your own is just getting the products to the consumers and earn your income. Whichever is the case, the terms determine the percentage of the proceeds you will take as commission. This type of business is suitable for job seekers as well as retirees. One sure thing is that there are many people looking for who will help sell their products. There are reasons for that:

Knowledge is increasing, inventions here and there. Hence there are many products or services that are meant to solve the same problem. There are substitutes everywhere. For any product to survive therefore, it requires aggressive marketing.

The population is on the increase, even rural areas are getting populated as cities are overpopulated already. All these people need to be reached with different products and services. This fact calls for sales and marketing.

The cost of marketing is another reason. Considering the number of marketing hands that will usually be required by producers and distributors, the traditional strategy of employing professional marketers will be too costly. Organizations are therefore looking for ways of selling their products with minimal personnel costs. That is now providing opportunities for marketers who are not professionals but have marketing as their hobby. If you are considering marketing other people's products, you are considering a business that is not only lucrative but also has very high potentials.

WHERE TO FIND PRODUCTS TO SELL
Trade shows, magazine, newspapers, and newsletters, online publications, exporters and manufacturers and importers manuals are good sources where to look for products to sell.

For trade shows and fairs, contact the chambers of commerce in your area. You can ask for calendar of upcoming trade shows that hold annually or periodically. You can directly contact manufacturers and suppliers asking for their wholesale prices and other conditions. Local library and book store of a university are good sources of business books, publications and trade magazines where you can get ideas of products you can sell.

HOW TO APPROACH SUPPLIERS AND MANUFACTURERS
Write a simple, cordial, yet professional letter to the principal

of the company such as Managing Director, Sales Director or Sales Manager, as the case may be. Ensure your letter is typed on computer or manually. Use your business letter heading (if you don't have, produce one, it costs very little).

You can also place a "product wanted" advertisement in a local newspaper or magazine and have suppliers contact you. Foreign trade sources are also good sources of new products. The internet can be of tremendous help in this case.

In any case, ensure you go for products that will give enough margins to cover your expenses. Select products you like from the sources you are confident in. When selecting which product to sell, make sure you choose the one you are proud of from the source you have confidence in. The source of the product must be the one that can motivate you.

SELLING INFORMATION PRODUCTS

We live in the era of information. Today, information is everywhere. Think of information books, magazines and journals on subject of public interest. Contact the publishers or authors on how you can distribute for them. One good thing about these information products is that they are mostly on sell or return basis. It simply means they will supply you on credit, you will sell and remit the money and also return the unsold copies. You have nothing to lose. It is a very good means of making cool money.

HOW TO FIND BUYERS
This will be the first thing to do. Look for buyers, people who need the products you are selling. In the case of information products, it is so easy. You only need to look for an audience that needs the information. Look for people who you know the information will help to solve their business or personal problems. Approach them, convince them and persuade them. The key here is that you must be interested in what you are selling. You must also have enough knowledge about your product and how it works. This will help you persuade other people.

In the case of tangible products, you look for companies and individuals that need the product for production or personal use. Feel free to approach them, tell them what you are selling. If it is a new product, tell them how it works. Get producers or manufacturers manual for them when this is necessary. If you approach some people and they reject your offer, never get discouraged.

HOW TO MAKE IT BIG WITH USED BOOKS
This business usually does not look very attractive until you take a look at the bank accounts of people that have been in it. The business is one of the small investment businesses; very good for beginners and those who are still holding other regular jobs. The type of person ideal for this business is one that loves reading, has read books over the years and likes associating with people of like minds.

Ideally, a used bookstore will need a market population of about 3000 persons to support it. You should therefore try to locate your store in a high traffic area, as near as possible to a college or a university campus. This is a business with a very high potential in Nigeria of today where secondhand or "Tokunbo" of every item is highly valued.

To have lots of sales, it is important that there be a lot of casual strollers in your location and that you encourage these people to drop in and browse around. Nigerians like to look around and see what they can benefit from any shop they pass. Most of these Nigerians have some change in their pockets that they would be willing to release to you for a good used book. The same goes for outdated magazines and journals.

Make your shop or counter attractive and display books in such a way that titles, author's names and subjects are easily seen.

Below is a list of the kinds of books you should consider stocking in used books store:
Business Books: included in this class are books on career, time management and people management and so on.

How To Books: these should include all the self help and self empowerment manuals you can find on mail order, auto repair, carpentry, metalwork, home building, gardening and business start up.

Special Interest Books: these are books on world war history, civil war, aviation, sports, perfection, movies and just plain old book collectors.

Internet Books: this is the rave of the moment and a lot of people are still ignorant about the use. They need books that tell about the use of the internet for business people, students, etc.

Paperbacks: books on science, fiction, romance, sexuality, mysteries and historical novels are in this category. I can bet it with you, these are good movers in our society of today.

Many used bookstores add to their income potentials by adding tape cassettes and lending libraries. These are real moneymakers with a kind of service that lend out books on purchase of the original tape cassettes. You can also add mail order book sales for more income. Many publishers and writers will be ready to give you these materials on sell or return basis. Only be ready to approach them with good confidence.

HOW TO START YOUR CATERING SERVICES IN A PROFITABLE WAY
In Nigeria of today, it is a way of proving your status and

STRAIGHT TO POINTS

displaying your affluence by making your social function a catered affair. Likewise, businesses of all sizes are using lunches, cocktail parties and dinner meetings to build their images and increase company sale. It is a matter of keeping up with the competition and promoting a company or its products. On a smaller but just as busy marketing scale, more and more working mothers are paying to have catered birthday and graduation parties as well as wedding receptions handled by caterers. The reasons are obvious. If she's working outside the home, today's mother just doesn't have time or the energy to do all the planning and staging of a memorable party. Caterers have everything from birthday parties for children, to breakfast in bed and intimate candle light dinner for two, to company dinner parties for 30 and wedding receptions involving a thousand or more guests. Most recognized associations and professional bodies make use of caterers for their dinners, luncheons and inductions. This type of entrepreneurial business is infinitely growing and becoming more popular with people of all income levels.

You don't need special education or training to become a successful caterer. You need an affinity for people and a kind of intuition to what people enjoy in different environmental settings. The business is even more ideal for an ambitious couple to start and operate with very little capital investment required. One person can spend his time hustling up business while the other would do the planning, organizing and actual catering. Understand exactly what your client wants and give him what he wants in a way of service that reflects upon the client in a complimentary manner.

GO FOR SMALL ADVERTISEMENT

Basically you can start with advertisement in your local news papers. This advertisement need not be much more than a simple announcement such as:

CREATIVE CATERING SPECIALIZING IN PERSONAL SERVICE – we can handle any party or special events from start to finish. No idea is too small or too large - your satisfaction is always guaranteed. Call us on 0803 ……………….. and let us make your party worth remembering.

You can also type your advertisement and past in public places like post office, banks, etc. That is, if you cannot afford the local newspaper advertisement.

RESPONSES FROM YOUR ADVERTS

The first thing you want to hear from anyone calling to ask about your service is that person's name, address and phone number. Then you want to know what kind of party or event he has in mind. As soon as you have this information, relax a little bit and enquire to find out about the person or the company or the people sponsoring the party and their ultimate goals or reasons for the party. You take the information you glean from this first interview and plan, organize the event on paper. This means you are going to have contacts or at least working relationships with innumerable service businesses, at least from your first successful outing. One thing is that if you perform creditably to the satisfaction of these people, they will book appointment with you. Always have your business cards with you. The initial capital you will need will majorly be in relation to kitchen utensils and serving materials. All these can also be rented.

MAKING HUGE PROFIT IN BAKERY BUSINESS

The unique magic of bread making is due to the interaction of the three main ingredients - wheat/flour, yeast and water. These are all about bread making; every other thing is optional and secondary. The special interaction of these ingredients is set off and controlled by the established steps of bread baking. As an excellent source of vitamins, protein and carbohydrates, bread has been an essential element of human diets for centuries all over the world.

The bread market is increasing by the day. It will continue to increase as people have less time to prepare raw food items in their homes. I may need to tell you that the market is becoming highly competitive these days because of the simplicity of the business of bread production. This notwithstanding, the bread industry is still almost virgin in many parts of Nigeria. There is real money you can make there.

The amount required to set up a bakery is directly related to the cash at hand. If you can, get a small parcel of land, about half a plot and build a clay oven. If you don't have a piece of land you can rent or look for an abandoned bakery for rent. Don't be scared, the fact that somebody abandoned his own does not change the fact that there is big money in the bakery business. It cost about N1,000,000.00 to start small, while it costs between N6,000,000.00 to N10,000,000.00 or more to start on a large scale. If you don't have enough money to buy all the equipment, you can hire for a particular duration with as little as N50,000.00.

BREAD MAKING EQUIPMENT

There are two major types of oven: they are clay oven and the fabricated oven. It will cost between N100,000.00 to N140,000.00 to mould a clay oven, while the fabricated oven will cost between N900,000.00 to N2,000,000.00, depending on the capacity.

Other equipment needed are milling machine, mixing machine, divider, molding machines, scales and pans. However, you can decide to go on a lower scale where your mixing is done with your hands in a basin, you use cupboard oven which could be bought for as low as N6,000.00 and the cutting and dividing is done with knife. At this capacity you may decide to choose a particular sales outlet, like banks where you can use interpersonal relations to sell your products to the staff.

There is real, good money in the bakery business. Your

success, however depends on the information available to you and the way you use the information. You can easily go to a bakery site and try to familiarize yourself with a bakery for a short time before commencing your own operation. Trial and error is very possible in learning the bakery business, but knowledge is profitable. You will need to learn about the risks involved in the business and how to avoid the avoidable. You also need to learn about staff management if you want to grow. Bakery business is labour intensive. Learn about how to obtain the needed credit to finance your bakery business. It is so easy.

PRODUCTION AND MARKETING OF FASHIONABLE HATS

It is a well-known fact that fashion is always evolving with new and innovative styles. There is no contesting the fact that the wearing of hats is one of the latest trends in fashion.

In churches, at weddings, at funerals and other occasions, on pages of magazines like Ovation and Empress, it is hats all over. You need to know that the use of hats is not for women only, men also use hats.

The Niger-Delta Nigerian men use hats very well. All these are to tell you that hats making business is a lucrative one and guarantees success throughout the year.

All that it requires is a capital of as low as N20, 000.00 and an in-depth training to acquire the skill. Surprisingly, you do the training in one day or a maximum of two days, if you are a slow learner.

All the businesses mentioned or discussed above will require knowledge and knowledge is freely available to people who value it. Always feel free to ask questions. You will also do well by trying to look for books, magazines and CDs on topics related to your business of interest. Even when you cannot buy, you can borrow, read and return.

NEWSPAPER CLIPPING SERVICE
Because newspaper clipping may sound new to many of us, I will adapt from the writing of expert on the business as follows:

This is a very lucrative business, and its growing in demand and popularity all over the world. There are thousands of people in parts of the world who are making hundreds of dollars each week, just reading, clipping news items in the privacy of their own homes!

The paper-clipping business is very much misunderstood by most people who are skeptical about it as a way for ordinary people to make extra money at home. If you explain to friends and neighbors that you operate a paper-clipping business, most of them will think you scan through the obituaries, funeral notices and wedding announcements, clipping these out and sending them to the people or relatives of the people being written about.

In reality, this is but a very small part of the home-based newspaper clipping service. Make contacts with companies and organizations that want to keep current on any number of matters reported in the newspapers about them.

Some companies abroad hire clipping services in order to keep track of what their competitors are doing. Other companies, including businesses of all kinds, use clipping services as a means of locating sales and new customers. National magazines and newspapers abroad are always in need of different or interesting materials, and frequently employ home-based clipping services.

To set yourself up in this kind of business here in Nigeria, you will need a pair of scissors and as many different newspaper and magazines as you can buy or subscribe to. A visit to some libraries around you should be most informative relative to newspapers and magazines available to subscribers. You can also meet with newspapers around you for opportunity of being a paying subscriber. This is not done presently in Nigeria, but you can be the one to start it. After all, many things that are done in Nigeria today were previously not done. They were all initiated by smart and innovative Nigerians.

You can also visit wholesale newspaper stands and make a deal with them. Visit your local vendors or state stationery store to buy labels at a discount price. You will want to attach these labels to the top of each clipping you send to your clients. On these labels, you will want to print the name of the publication the clipping came from, the date it appeared, as well as your own name and address.

The next step is simply to start clipping articles that mention or talk about specific companies or people. File your clippings in envelopes or boxes according to industries or types of business, by company name, and according to names of the people mentioned.

Once you have ten or more clippings that talk about a particular company or person, put them in an envelope and send them to that company's owner or public relations director.(*I recommend you go in person*). You should include a short note with the clippings, explaining your service and your fee.

You should try and get your clients to agree to pay you a monthly "reader's fee", for which you agree to look for anything in the newspaper about him or his company or industry. Every time you spot such an article, you of course clip it and send it to him. A minimum of monthly "reader's fee" is usually about $25 in the U.S. but it can vary according to the number of clipping found. So here in Nigeria you can charge as much as you want to (*depending on the company or person involved*).

Generally, a clipping service abroad scans State-wide publications will charge about $50 per client, or $100 per client for those wanting clippings from national publications. These fees, of course, are monthly fees, and you can easily see how you could make some very good money with just 20 to 25 clients

To promote and build your business, you can scan your local or state business services directory and make out a solicitation letter to each of those listed. A couple of days after you have posted your sales letter; you should follow up with a phone call or visit.

A short to-the-point advertisement in the state or national daily will also bring in new clients for you like a small display advert in the yellow pages of your telephone directory.

You should definitely contact the public relations firms, advertising agencies and civic organizations in your area. Explain your services and ask them if they have any special clients or needs you can help them with. You will find many of your political and "course" groups very interested in receiving clippings about their opponents. Election time can be very delicate point in our country and this newspaper clipping business idea works very well in such circumstances. A lot of things are being said about lots of politicians. Certainly, our rich and influential Nigerian politicians would definitely want to know what is being said or not being said about them in the states and national dailies by people all over the country. And of course, they will not have time to sift through all the state and national dailies in the country to find it out. Do this 'stress-less working from home' for them and earn a whole lot of money.

You can come up with an advert in any of the dailies with something like this:

ATTENTION / POLITICAL CANDIDATES FOR 2015 (or any other) ELECTIONS (SENATORS! HOUSE OF REP MEMBERS! GOVERNORS! PRESIDENTIAL CANDIDATES, ETC)

2015 elections are around the corner! Are you among the players? Do you know what the newspapers are saying or not saying about you? With all the newspaper and magazines in and outside the country, there is just no way for you to know. Face it; you have lots of other things to do. Let us do the dirty job for you. Let us search EVERYDAY, through the national and state newspapers and magazines for you to find out what is being said or not being said about you. This is our JOB. Let us do it for you!!
For more information, contact:…………………………......
Phone: ………………………………………………….........

The idea is very workable. All you have to do is to let the workability of it sink down into your head and let your subconscious mind come up with the 'how and who'? and you are on your way to another 'work from home' opportunity to make lots and lots of money.

Clipping services as money making ventures, in one form or another, have been around in most countries of the world since the advent of printing press and they are becoming more in demand. It's definitely the kind of business anyone who knows how to read can set up and operate with an absolute minimum investment.

The good news is that everything about news paper clipping nowadays can be done electronically online.

AUTHORITATIVE INFORMATION BROKING
Information is said to be the most expensive thing that sells in the world today. Though, it is free at most times to get information, this doesn't mean that people will not pay money for it. Also, many people can't go through the stress of searching for information they need. They, therefore pay other people to do this work. To make money finding the information that people need is quite easy, whether you are a writer or not. When you are doing research or looking for information on a particular subject, it's a lot like a detective checking all his possible clues. The important thing is knowing who or where you source the information from.

STRAIGHT TO POINTS

In almost all instances, your first move should be your encyclopedia. If you don't have an up-to-date set, there's always your public library. In Nigeria, the public libraries are seriously under-utilized. There are lots of information in most of the public libraries around, make use of them.

Most of the time, an encyclopedia will give you at least the general facts about your subject. You may have to check other sources for more detailed information.

Thus, your next move should be to books that have been written on the subject. The subject and title sections of the card catalogue or the bound volumes of the computer print outs in most of the public libraries will give you plenty of listings.

After you have selected a number of books for background information, check the magazines either directly related to your subject, or those carrying articles on the subject. Most of the time, you will find that magazines will provide you with more up-to-date and timely information than books.

To check out information on your subject in magazines, look in the Reader's Guide to Periodical Literature. Under the subject and author headings, the complete collection of this guide will list articles printed in magazines since the turn of the century. The suggestions for use section will instruct you on how to read the codes under each head. If you can't find your subject listed, think of similar or closely related subjects.

If your subject is part of a particular field of study, there may be a special index that will help you. Among these special indexes, you will find: Art Index, Business Periodicals Index, Social Sciences Index, Biological and Agricultural Index and Applied Sciences and Technology Index. You may also find a popular periodical Index that lists articles that have appeared in currently popular magazine.

And most newspapers are very good as reference materials. Special national newspapers abroad, such as the Wall Street Journal, also have reference indexes. Without a doubt, the New York Times Index is the most complete. In these newspaper indexes, subjects and people are listed alphabetically with the date, page, number and the likes.

The internet would also be very useful in giving you all you need on your subject matter. Most newspapers, magazines and journals usually available on their publisher's website long after they no longer exist on the vendors' table.

One thing about this idea, which makes it easier, is that you are not, neither are you purporting to be the source of the information you are providing. You need to quote and blend information from different sources on a particular subject.

You need to decide on the form your information would be packaged. This would naturally depend on the audience and your available resources. Whichever way, I can assure you that you have the money in it to make. You may never imagine how much money the writers are making from most pamphlets and hand books on current affairs. Depending on the nature, the blend and the depth of information you provide, you may have to obtain copyright for your work. To do this, there is a minimum amount of information you can collect from a copyrighted source to avoid piracy.

BULLETIN BOARD ADVERTISING SERVICES

Bulletin boards actually work as traffic builders for just about any small business. They serve to enhance the community relation's image of the business, and the space required to locate a bulletin board might not even cost you anything.

Just take your time and go through this book and you will know what I am talking about, and how you can take advantage and make money with it.

Bulletin boards are important because people use the "business provided" bulletin boards to advertise things they want to sell, home based business and whatever they might want to trade for or buy. Then, they come back, sometimes morning or noon, and evening every day, to check on them, or to see who else has an announcement posted. Each time they come into the business owner's store or shop, they may not feel an obligation to buy something, but of course the business owner has another opportunity to sell something.

Just about anybody can organize a route of bulletin boards, charge the advertisers a small monthly fee, keep them up-to-date and make easy money in the process.

The first step is to contact as many businesses in your area as possible. Superstores, pharmacies, barber shops, beauty salons, service stations, print shops, rental shops, shopping centers, places that have sports and recreation rooms and the list is endless.

Sell them the idea of allowing you to install and maintain a bulletin board service for them. Emphasize the community service, the tax write-off, and the fact that you will keep it neat. When you get ten or more signed to allow you to install a bulletin board, you are ready to start making your bulletin boards.

The best plan (and of course the most economical) is to make your own. Cut a piece of chalkboard 3 feet by 4 feet, mount ¾ by 1-inch frame around the edge, and cover this frame with a 3 feet by 4 feet piece of plastic. Mount the plastic with hinges at the top and a hasp at the bottom. On the back of the chalkboard, install a couple of hooks for hanging it and you are ready to go.

Make up a sign - you can even type it out and use it as another bulletin board announcement - something like this:

STATE WIDE BULLETIN BOARD SERVICES!
Your announcement or advertisement displayed here for only N1,000 per month! For more information call............... Or contact ………..

Put your sign or announcement on each of your bulletin boards, lock them up, and install them in all your locations. Ten of such signs with only 5 announcements per bulletin board should bring you an easy N50,000 per month!

When you put an announcement from the same person up or more than one board, charge them N1,000 per month for each announcement on each bulletin board. And one other thing: the date the "run of display" ends should be marked on each announcement you put on each of your boards.

In all likelihood, you may have people waiting for space on your bulletin boards. Start with a loose-leaf notebook, blank paper and a couple of packages of 5 by 5 cards. In your notebook, write down the date, the amount of money received and the number of announcements on display, and the contract expiration date. On the 3 by 5 cards write the name, address, phone number and expiration date of each contract, and the locations of the bulletin boards that particular announcement is on. Arrange the cards in chronological order according to expiration date, and file them in a storage box.

Once you get rolling, you shouldn't have to service your bulletin boards more than once a week, and more people see them, more businesses will want you to put one in their business location, and more people will want to display an announcement. This is simple, easy, and a real money-maker for you, no matter the state in Nigeria that you are located. Be sure your boards are sighted in strategic locations like general hospital, motor parks, shopping mall, government secretariats, universities, polytechnic and college campuses.

This kind of business is what our Nigeria newspapers like to write about, and the TV stations like to carry as news of what people in their areas are doing as entrepreneurs. So, take the feature editors out to lunch, make friends with them, and push for all the free publicity you can get.

That's the plan. It's simple, easy and depending upon the population density of your area, it could very well be the very thing you have been looking for to supply you an extra income. It demands little investment, not much of your time, and any special training or education. However, as with any business venture, it takes ACTION on your part. You must get out there and set it up, and work at making it a success for you! It's really up to you.

BUMPER STICKER SERVICES

One of the things central to any business is advertisement. No business can make reasonable progress without engaging in one form of advert or the other. And as a result of this, adverts are becoming more and more expensive, especially big media adverts like those on T.V, radio, newspapers, etc.

Many companies and businesses are constantly looking for cheaper and yet 'effective' advertisement options. You can make lots of money if you can provide a cheap but effective way of advertising for these individuals and organizations. But this time, it is advertising with car bumper stickers.

As you consider this idea for a source of income, your first decision will be whether to first line up people willing to "wear" the bumper stickers on their cars, or the business owners who will want to pay you, for you to advertise them in this manner.

One person who started such a business years ago in US, found it easier to sell to a business owner by telling him that 100 to 200 people were all set and willing to wear his bumper sticker advertisement, because such people were known by him to be in the area.

This boils down to a recommendation that you talk to your friends, neighbors and co-workers first. Get as many of them as you can to agree to "wear" a bumper sticker. You might offer to pay N100 (*depends on what you can profit from those who will pay you to set this kind of advert for them*) for three months or N50 for six weeks. With inducement of money just to put a bumper sticker on their cars or trucks, you won't have too many turn down. Many will be glad to be paid by you for just wearing ordinary bumper sticker. Many will even think you are crazy to contemplate paying them just to have them wear your bumper sticker, especially the commercial bus drivers plying most of our roads all over Nigeria.

This is an ideal business for constant free publicity write-ups in your local newspaper, plus interviews on radio and TV talk shows. At first, you will want as many people as possible to "wear" bumper sticker adverts. What you will want in any publicity write-up or media interviews is the fact that you got the "vehicle for exposure" lined up and organized so that any potential advertiser needs only to give you a call or contact you, and you can launch his advertising programme immediately.

Next, you check with a number of printers and determine the cost to have bumper stickers made to order. Generally, you should be able to get a thousand bumper stickers for N2500 or less, depending on the kind of stickers and the state you reside in. Whatever the cost, this initial outlay should be absorbed by your charge to the advertiser.

So, let's suppose you have 100 people lined up to "wear" one of these bumper stickers on their cars for six weeks. Figure the bumper stickers will cost N1,000. Now, it comes to the problem of what to charge the advertiser.

You should always charge on a "per car" basis i.e., on a basis of circulation, as newspaper do. So, you could charge N50 or more, depending on you, the advertiser and the state and circumstances surrounding you, per car, per week, with 100 cars. This comes to N5000 per week or N30, 000 totals over six weeks, from the advertiser. Subtract N1000 for getting the bumper sticker made, say N4, 000 as payment to cars "wearing" the bumper stickers and you would end up with a profit picture of N25, 000 for those six weeks. This is just a conservative example of potentials of the business. You can charge whatever you like so far as it is workable in your area. Politicians, religious organizations, NGOs and government agencies use this type of advertisement.

In the beginning, you should be the one calling on potential advertisers and doing all the selling. Once you have your first programmes organized and running smoothly, your next step is a natural multiplication of your efforts.

This kind of advert has been debated all over the world as very effective because it is advert in motion. In other words, the advert goes to people and not the other way round. Unlike radio or TV advert, you don't have to put it on to view or hear it. You have to sit down and enumerate the advantages of this type of business so that you will convince whoever wants to advertise with you why this method will do wonders for him or her.

It's easy! It's simple! And it works! Compared to other more traditional advertising methods, bumper sticker advertising is very low in cost. One of the tricks of the trade is in using short, snappy, even humorous slogans or telegram styled messages. Another idea is to make the lettering on the bumper sticker luminous to the headlights of the cars following. Most importantly, be sure to make your lettering easy to read, and the message easy to comprehend at one glance.

With a great dose of imagination and determination, you probably will never run out of places ready to be sold on your plan of bumper sticker advertising.

The important things are to always be creative in your selling efforts. Always show the prospect how his business can grow from advertising in the manner you propose, and how your method is more positive, more responsive, and lower in cost than the more traditional advertising.

Remember, too, the cleverer or "catchy" the message on the bumper sticker, the more it will make people talk and respond.

Remember also that advertising is a form of "brainwashing" and the more people see the message, the stronger the message is imprinted in their minds. Therefore, when they need or are in the market for the services or product offered by the advertiser, they will quickly refer to the strongest, easiest-to-recall advertising message in their minds. And that, of course, means that if the prospect sees a specific advertising message on the bumper of the cars in front of him day after day, when he's ready to buy, that particular advertiser will be the one he will patronize.

You can expand this business to include magnetic signs on the cars, saddle-back signs on the back of cars, and even signs in the yards in residential neighborhoods.

CONSULTANCY SERVICES

Business is all about the exchange of goods or services for money. It is just becoming clear to the people in the business world that selling services is more profitable than selling goods. One, most services don't have fixed prices; what you charge depends on you and the recipient of your services. Most goods have either fixed prices or fixed range of prices. Two, there is less competition in the service market. All over the world, services are always in short supply. Medical profession and medical services has been known in our country for centuries now, yet it is still in short supply. If you are interested in current affairs, you would have heard that since the return of democracy, the Nigerian government has been working relentlessly to ensure the number of medical and paramedical personnel in Nigeria is increased to cope with the health challenges of our population. Fourteen years are passed there is still the short supply of medical personnel all over the nation.

When we were still students of the Institute of Chartered Accountants of Nigeria (ICAN), majority of us assumed that the Council of the Institute doesn't want many people to pass the examinations, so that we would not have too many Chartered Accountants. Now that we have passed the examinations, and have joined the Chartered colleagues, we have come to know better and differently. Do you know that Chartered Accountants are still in short supply in Nigeria, with less than 50,000 (Fifty Thousand) Chartered Accountants. The same thing is applicable to other professions. Lawyers are in short supply, architects are not enough, estate surveyors are wanted everywhere. Teachers, Lecturers, Engineers, Technicians, Pastors, musicians and humanitarian service providers are needed all over the country.

But some of these people are still jobless, you may want to ask? The reason for that is very simple. It is because many of these people do not understand the service concept. In our schools and colleges, they don't teach much about services. The only type of services that we prepare people for in our education system is the service of employment. Just open your eyes and mind you will see services needed around you which you can conveniently offer and make plenty money.

Three, service is flexible and adaptive. There are hundreds of services you can engage in right from the comfort of your home, even while you still maintain a paid job. Some services can go almost effortlessly to faraway places without the physical presence of the owner or provider. When I published my first book, I was surprised about two months later when somebody came to tell me how he saw my book in Mubbi, Adamawa State. Yet, I did not have any distributor or agent around that zone of the country. In fact, as at that time, I only sold in the south eastern states of Nigeria. We have been able to package our services in such a way that generations after us can conveniently benefit from it. Some tangible products have that features too, but in case of tangible goods, extra efforts and cost would certainly be involved. There are services you can offer using telephone conversations. There are services you can offer using radio or television medium. There are services you can offer through newspaper, magazines and journals. Even if you advertised your goods through the media your personal contact or that of your representative will usually be needed to make the sales.

Four, a good service is always very unique, it cannot be perfectly imitated. Good services are actually a reflection of the personality offering it. And by nature, every single human being on earth is unique.

QUALIFICATIONS

One way to package services that will put good money in your pocket is that of consultancy services. When I talk about consultancy, many people will think until you get a professional certificate before you can engage in consultancy services. Although, there are regulated services which require you having a professional certificate and at times a practicing license before you can dabble into them, but there are many services you can provide without belonging to a particular professional body. Of course, your degree certificate, NCE certificate and technical certificate are all there for you to practice with. I remember when I was to register my business with Corporate Affairs Commission some years back, one particular thing that was queried was the fact that I wrote consultancy as one of the services my business would be providing. You know what? I intentionally did not put my professional certificates there initially. I did that just to establish a point. At the end of the day I was asked to present a certificate to support the fact that I wanted to provide consultancy services. I simply asked what type of certificate they needed. You may be surprised that they said I could bring my degree certificate. Even though I chose to use a professional certificate, my degree could still serve the purpose. When your university or polytechnic awarded you a certificate at the end of your four or five year's course, the certificate was not only to look for job. It is also to provide services and provide jobs for other people.

THINK SERVICES, MONEY WILL COME TO YOU
I remember a building contractor I met some years ago. The man is a big time contractor. He is a native of Oyo State based in Lagos, but takes contracts all over the nation. At least, we met in Imo State where he was executing a chain of contracts for a particular rich man. He constructed a magnificent business complex, two modern standard petrol stations, one international secondary school complex and another country home residence for the same man. Even though he lives with his family in Lagos, He had built, magnificent personal house in Ibadan. He has three cars, one of them is a SUV. He has trained almost all his children in school and he has many share certificates which he does not even know what to do with them except the collection of his dividends ones in a while. He gave me his business card and his title is "Engineer". So, his name is Engineer so and so. People simply call him Engineer. He has many labourers working for him.

You know one surprising thing about this man? He did not attend any university or polytechnic. From our discussion, I got to know that he did not have more than elementary education. Yet, he is a consultant in that field. He only learnt building construction - what our people call brick laying under an apprenticeship and then developed himself, built relationships and connections. If an illiterate is consulting, how much more you, a graduate. The man I am talking about is working for highly educated people and making money more than you can imagine. His services are good, and then his clients have ignored his educational background. At least, the man he was working for when I met him was a retired Comptroller of customs, who would later become a member of federal house of representatives. Imagine that.

CONSULTANCY IS NEEDED EVERYWHERE

Why must you consider consultancy as a means of money generation? The opportunity is enormous. Even in the areas of life where you can almost ignore, consultancy is needed there. A friend of mine is a consultant on bakery matters. If you want to set up a bakery business, or you have problem managing an existing bakery, he would help you out. With that, you know it is not only accountants or doctors that can consult. My friend read Food Science and Technology, then worked in a bakery and later worked in a flour mill as a sales person. Now, he is able to put his knowledge and experience together to make as much money as he wants. He recommends good materials to the bread and confectionery manufacturers and he does the supply.

KNOWLEDGE IS THE PRODUCT.

In consultancy service, what you are selling is knowledge. And that establishes another reason why services sell more than goods. Because knowledge is immeasurable and limitless, services sell more than goods. The same knowledge can serve millions of people, even at the same time. No goods can do that. If you have used your knowledge for thousands of people, instead of the knowledge reducing, it will rather increase. All you need is to renew your knowledge day by day by expression, accumulation and application; it will always remain to make all the money you want.

MEET THIS MAN

My uncle is a consultant without a business name. You know his area of specialization? He is a consultant in political matters. When it comes to politics, in the whole of our constituency, he is now a king maker. If you want to win election simply consult him. If you want to lose, all you need is ignore his ideas. You know what? My uncle is not an illiterate, but he is not educated. You know what I mean? At least, I know he has been in this business since 1979 to date. He might have been there long before that, but at least that is the little I know. The highly educated and rich people who are contesting elections consult him on strategies and campaign. He was in the team that worked for Chief Bola Ige in Oyo State in 1979. In 1983, he worked for Dr. Omololu Olounloyo and in 1991 for Chief Isiaka Adeleke in Osun State and so on up till date. Why do I need to bother you about my uncle's affair? The reason is simple. I just want to show you how you don't need all the formal education and school certificates before you can start making money as a consultant. I will show you how my uncle conducts his affairs and naturally generates money for himself and his family.

Most of the time, my uncle would sit down discussing politics for hours either in a formal meeting or just general discussion among his people. That may continue for about fourteen hours a day. He makes sure he updates himself in all the theories and philosophy of the Nigerian political heroes like Obafemi Awolowo, Nnamdi Azikwe and people like Abraham Lincoln of the United States of America. You can't listen to him and not be carried away, even if you are in the opposition party. The only thing you can do is avoid listening to him at all. If you tried listening to him, you may end up joining his party in a matter of days. My observation is this. Most times, the man would sit down talking like that till 11.00pm or 12.00 midnight. Yet, he has current newspapers waiting for him in the room. Any time he closes from the talk or meeting, he would go through those papers cover to cover. He would read all stories that are of particular interest to him. He may sleep by 3.00 am; he just must read to prepare himself for the following morning. It is from the papers and books he prepares himself for the next day. He simply ensures that he has enough information on politics and he is selling it to people for their money.

HOW TO GO ABOUT IT
You need to develop yourself. Gather enough knowledge in an area of life. It is advisable you carefully select such an area in accordance with your natural gifts and the people's need. Registration of business with Corporate Affairs Commission is necessary, but you can make a lot of money before you register. In fact, the business finances itself. It is from your first services that you will register your business, whatever form you want it to be. Stationeries like letter heading,

invoices, receipts, etc are very important. But you can make a lot of money before you buy stationeries, because the business is all about relationship and trust. It is also about your ability to convince people about yourself and your service. An office accommodation is very important, but you can start making profit before getting office accommodation. You can do it right from your house where you reside. You can do it while still working with your employer. The only thing is that you need to avoid conflict of interests and unfaithfulness to your employer. To do that, you only need to prepare your mind for extra time of work. If your paid job is 8.00am to 4.00pm (8 hours), you simply have to prepare you mind for extra two to four hours work each day. The truth is that, the extra two to four hours you put into your private venture may give you more money than your eight hours employment.

Equipment like computer, telephone line, furnitures and the likes are very important, but you can start without them. You can do consultancy services as full time or part time business. Members of the National Youth Service Corp (NYSC) can also do it. As a corps member, it has to be on part time basis because of your primary assignment. But don't forget that many corps members are posted to places where they do nothing or next to nothing each day. Most government offices especially the local government, have no single assignment for corpers.

The areas in which you can consult are numerous. Areas of

Accountancy, Book Keeping, Agriculture, Marketing, Engineering, Medicine, Pharmaceuticals, Teaching, Management, Human resources, Investment, Construction, Fabrication, Mechanical and so on are all full of opportunity for Consultancy Services. Computer Science, Information and Communication Technology and Internet have provided our world with a modern gold mine. Take advantage of them.

TELEVISION AND RADIO PRODUCTION
First of all, I need to tell you that this is one of the business opportunities with the highest possible business returns but are reserved for people who can generate some initial capital. It is in the same class with film/video production and marketing. There is so much money to make in these areas than anybody can imagine.

When you are doing this type of money making activities, people would never assume you are out to make yourself rich. They would see you as doing community or humanitarian services. They would see you as a young social individual who is using his or her natural gifts and talent to benefit the society. And so people would freely do business with you and part with their money for your services than they would do for any other person. If you are from a rich or wealthy family, this is one of the areas you can put your parents' money and multiply your family wealth forever.

Radio and Television are means of communication whereby people express themselves and share their ideas with others.

Advancement in technology has created abundant opportunities in this area for almost everybody. Nigeria currently has about 160 television stations. Some of these belong to the Federal and State Government while a good number are owned by individuals and business organizations. We have over 200 radio stations spread all over the country and all of them are potential goldmine not only for the station owners but also for young enterprising people like you.

Nigeria currently has the largest television and radio network in Africa and this has provided for healthy competition. Whatever is the theme and focus of the programs, there is an advantage of deep traditions of the over 1000 cultural groups which make up Nigeria. We are also influenced by numerous global cultures whose products and aesthetics bombard Nigerian daily through the airwaves. All these provide unlimited opportunities to make big money through the electronic media.

TYPES OF PROGRAMMES
There are current affairs issues that are news oriented and programmes that are critically fictional. There are sports programmes, automobiles, information technologies, telecommunications, shoppers guide, maritime, politics, aviation, general education, health, family, finance, insurance, musical, fashion, hospitality, religion, real estate, dating, school quiz, children and teenagers' programmes, agriculture and women empowerment. The list is endless.

You have to make choice considering your personal interest and hobbies, your finance and your targeted audience. You can produce or compose jingles for companies, government and even television and radio stations. If your composition is good they will certainly pay you good money.

These programs can be packaged by you and turned into a million naira air programs, with sponsors competing to pay you for it.

PRODUCTION PROCESS

It takes the same process to package these programmes for radio and television production. Basically, every programmes must have particular objectives. It must revolve around a concept or an idea. As a young graduate, depending on your background, it is important to tailor your programmes towards your educational background, inclination of your natural gift and interest. Irrespective of the different types of programmes, the methodology for packaging them for television and radio is similar.

Basically, there are three stages involved to get your production to the point of putting money in your pocket.

1. STAGE ONE:

This stage could be called pre-production stage. The first step is for you to have an idea, and then develop it into a script for shooting or packaging the programmes.

1. Decide on number of presenters required.

2. Decide whether it should be a live programme or a recorded programme.

3. Whether interviews or musicals would be involved

4. Whether there would be any commercial and backup.

5. Is it a collaborative arrangement with the station or an independent programme that would be sponsored by you or your sponsor?

It is also important for you to make a budget. This will help you determine the cost involved and possibly help when you are looking for sponsors.

STAGE TWO
This is where you will go out to do the recording. You must make sure that everything is near perfection, even if you have to do the recording over and over again. If you cannot do the recording alone, try to engage a consultant. When your idea is unique, the risk of it been duplicated by other people involved would be minimal. You, however need to consider the protection of your idea in selecting the consultant to use. Give priority to integrity. If the programme is going to be a live programme, what you need is practice not recording.

STAGE THREE
This is the editing stage, when you will go to the studio to edit. It is here you will select the most important part of what you have recorded and exclude the ones that are not very relevant. You must reduce the whole thing to fall in line with the time available to you.

MAKING MONEY AS AN INDEPENDENT PRODUCER
As an independent producer, you pay for the time to air your programme, then welcome people and organisations to place their advertisements, paying you good money in return. If your programme is rich in terms of content and it is widely accepted, you are bound to make money that exceeds your wildest imagination. You can reproduce the same programme on other radio and television stations. All would ultimately give you fat cash.

PARTNER WITH TV OR RADIO STATIONS.
If you have a very good programme, television and radio stations are ready to give you free air time pending the time the sponsors will come in. One thing is sure, if your programme is good and rich, sponsors will definitely come. All you need is packaging your programme very well. Make sure it is in line with the norms, trends and fashion of the society. Then feel free to approach the Radio and Television station authorities.

There are many TV and Radio stations looking for quality programmes that corporate organisations can sponsor. These organisations are looking for audience appealing programme where they can insert their adverts and the TV stations are also looking for programmes that these organizations can sponsor. If you are from the western part of Nigeria, you probably would remember programs like; Iriri Aye, Nkan mbe, Feyikogbon and the likes. You remember how many people waited expectantly for these programs each week. Super Story is also a good example of a program that millions of Nigerians await expectantly each week. Multimillion organisations would usually rush to have their advertisements placed during such a show.

DOCUMENTARY CLIP PRODUCTION
Documentary clip production is the biggest money making opportunity here available. You can just do a rundown of an activity that will interest the public. It could be political, business, investment or educational in nature. Anyone you chose, you are bound to make fat money.

Where do you sell your documentary? Channels TV stations have always been in the forefront of showcasing documentary between their news and programmes. Well produced documentary of a state government or company can be shown during this period. The government or the company would then pay you for it.

TALK SHOW CLIP
Talk shows are major profit making angle of TV business. It is a boom in the United States and other Western nations. The opportunity is very open in Nigeria as well. Make sure the topic like the Niger Delta problem, 2015 general elections, election petition, tribunal verdicts, naira redenomination, constitution amendment, election in the United States of America, world cup championship, impeachment proceedings and third term agenda can be discussed with the main people involved making it lively and fun to enjoy.

BUSINESS CLIP
This area is very interesting and profitable. However, you must be very innovative to make it here. You can package people's businesses and let them pay for it and then find a TV station that will share the profit with you for showing the clips.

REALITY CLIPS
In these days of sophisticated camera phone and visual shorter devices, you can get real live scenario of people's activities and get their permission to show it on TV. You could tell them it is their social responsibility to the public to make them excited and bring life to their homes and family. It can be fun. Definitely sponsors will come running for your programme.

MANAGING THE TRANSITION

10

I assume majority of people starting personal business are people already engaged in one activity or the other. Usually, most people move from the world of employment to the world of business and entrepreneurship. For some, it is a transition from passive investment to active investment. Passive investors are people who put their money in other people's businesses without their own personal involvement. They do this via investment in shares through the capital market, private placement or partnership arrangement. Some keep their money in different money market instruments, awaiting different rates of return. All of these are passive investors or passive business people.
I have been involved in both sides of the divide and I can tell

the difference. However, what this book emphasizes is active business. Your entire being is involved. You take active risks with your money and your talents. You also take risk with other people's money and other people's talents. Hence, it involves a complete change of what you do and what you are. It requires, also a change of thinking and orientation and often times, a change of association. Therefore, this is actually a transition that cannot be treated casually.

We must also recognize the fact that there are people who move from active role, usually part ownership in an existing business, to their own private business. There are others, who move directly from school or from apprenticeship to personal business. Even this class of people must acknowledge they are in a transition.

There is the question of when is the right time to transit? There is no single answer for this question because the right time depends on you and your circumstances. It depends on your mindset, your orientation and your long term plan. I have heard people saying it depends on how much they have. To such people I can say categorically, money, even though an important factor, is a secondary factor to any serious minded start up. I personally believe you cannot start too early. The real question is, whether you are personally prepared for the real world of business. Rather than the fear of starting too early, people should be afraid of starting too late.

EVERYBODY IN BUSINESS
Earlier in this book, I have talked about the reaction of one respected business man to the content of my first book. His question was that, if everybody practices what was taught in my book, then who will remain as an employee to work for the business owners? There will still be millions of employees all over the world. Employer of today was once an employee. Millions of employers of tomorrow are currently employees with different organisations. The only difference is that employment will rather be what people enjoy as against what they endure. There will be mutual respect between employers and employees.

Employees will become more productive because they will be people who are happy doing what they do. Employers will appreciate them more and motivate them better. It will result in a win-win situation.

BECOMING A BUSINESS MAN
Another question is whether everybody can be or become business person or an entrepreneur. The answer is yes and no. This question could mean a lot of things. It is no because people asking this question normally refer to whether everyone possesses natural talents, gifts or personal traits of an entrepreneur. These people believe that success in business has more to do with your natural gifts or talents.

Natural ability and talents do help in business. So, if you look at it from the angle of natural talents, not everybody has the concentration of gifts and talents required for business success. That is where my 'no' answer above comes from. It is, however important to note that possession of natural ability or gift is not enough for business success. No one has ever achieved lasting success in business and entrepreneurship simply because he is naturally gifted. Check other areas of human endeavors, you will discover that there has never been and there will never be anyone that achieved long time success based on natural talents alone.

Gifts, talents and temperament are important to success in any human endeavor. But what we call gifts, talents, temperaments and emotions are what is available in everybody at different levels of concentration. You have a particular gift simply because there is a dominance of the traits that make up that gift in you. The other person who is regarded is not possessing that gift is the one that has those trait, but not in a dominant proportion.

In addition, there are two sources to every gift or talent. The first source is **endowment**. You just grew up and found yourself with such ability by nature. The second source is **development**. This has to do with the development of those traits which are either dominant or non dominant in you. And all the gifts you celebrate in other people are actually present in you, at least in a non dominant proportion. The interesting thing is that all these can be cultivated and developed.

I must conclude here by stating that successful people in life are more products of development and cultivation than endowments and gifts. This is the reason for my yes answer above. Wisdom is for you to determine what is most important to you in life and develop yourself along that line. No one, therefore should bother himself on whether he is destined to be a successful business man or not. One should rather be bothered about whether or not he is prepared to be a successful business person. This preparation has physical, emotional, intellectual, social, financial and even spiritual dimensions.

ROBERT KIYOSAKI IN ENGLISH LANGUAGE
If you are familiar with the world of business and advocacy for financial literacy, you must have read or at least heard about Robert Kiyosaki. He is the author of the best seller **"Rich Dad Poor Dad"**.

Since Rich Dad Poor Dad was published in 1997, both the book and the author have become celebrated in the world of personal finance in America and the world. Without attempting to advertise Robert or his book, permit me to quote his comments about rich dad poor dad in his latest book **"Why 'A' Students Work for 'C' Students and 'B' Students Work for the Government"** published in 2013.

"In the year 2000, Rich Dad Poor Dad made the New York Times Best Sellers List, the only self-published book on

the list at that time. Then Oprah Winfrey called. I went on her television show and the "Oprah effect" took over.

Rich Dad Poor Dad has become the number one personal finance book of all time. It was on the New York Times Best Sellers list for over six years. To date, it has sold over 30 million copies worldwide, has been published in 53 languages and is available in 109 countries."

This author must be a very remarkable person. Of course, Rich Dad Poor Dad was first published in English Language in the United States of America in 1997 before being translated to 52 other languages across the globe. I also know other books written and publish by Robert since 1997.

Am I out to recommend Robert Kiyosaki's books? Yes. I recommend his books for all my readers particularly those who want to learn lessons on personal finance and entrepreneurship, such as are not learnt in today's formal educational institutions. But I actually mean more than recommending his books. I want to draw a lesson from the next paragraph of his books **"Why 'A' Students Work for 'C' Students and 'B' Students Work for Government"** I quote him in the following paragraph:

"The irony is, I failed English twice in the high school. I failed because I could not write, could not spell, and because the teacher did not agree with what I was writing."

What made a student, who failed English language, at least twice, to become a best seller author? And his bestselling books are not writing in another language. He writes in English and through business sense he gets others to translate to other languages. What really made a bad English student of yesterday a bestselling author of today? Training, learning, and personal development. With proper mindset for business, you can learn all other things you require for business success. What you cannot learn you can buy. Learning in itself is buying. Learning means you use your available resources to buy knowledge.

MANAGING THE TRANSITION
In his 2009 book, What Americans really want ... really, Dr. Frank Luntz, a respected pollster who measures the heartbeat of America, asked this survey question:

If you had to choose, would you prefer to be a business owner or CEO of a fortune 500 company?

Those questioned responded as follow:
80% want to be owner of a business that employs 100 or more people.

14% want to be CEO of a Fortune 500 Company that employs more than 10,000 people.
6% don't know or refused to answer.
In other words, majority of today's employees would like to

become entrepreneurs. Majority want their freedom. Dr. Luntz found that over 70% of full time, corporate employees are considering or have considered starting their own businesses. Many people dream of becoming entrepreneurs, but few take the real steps to realize their dreams. What actually is the problem? Fear of transition. Fear of the unknown. Most employees are afraid of losing their jobs. They are afraid of month end without a paycheck. There is the fear of taking the risk. The reality is that not taking risk itself is risky. Some of the disappointment and maltreatment you face even in employment, particularly in low wage countries, are enough to tell us that it is risky to perpetually leave your future in the hands of an employer.

Rather than allowing fear to keep you in bondage, learn to manage the transition period. Managing the transition requires learning and equipping yourself with the right mindset even before you set out. It also requires you knowing when to quit your paid job, if you currently hold one. Even though time can never be ripe enough to avoid all the challenges of a start up, your wisdom to prepare and your level of preparation can help a long way. Never attempt to wait for a perfect time. But use every opportunity to prepare yourself mentally, emotionally, intellectually, financially and spiritually.

MICROSOFT OFFICE BOY
I read the following story recently and I think I should share it:

A jobless man applied for the position of office boy at Microsoft. The HR manager interviewed him then watched him cleaning the floor as a test. "You are employed", he said.

Give me your e-mail address and I will send you the application to fill in, as well as date when you may start. The man replies, "But I don't have a computer; neither an email". "I am sorry" said the manager. "If you don't have an email that means you do not exist. And who doesn't exist cannot have the job."

The man left with no hope at all. He didn't know what to do, with only $10 in his pocket. He then decided to go to the Mbare Musika and bought a 10kg tomato crate. He sold the tomatoes in a door to door round. In less than 2 hours, he succeeded to double his capital. He repeated the operation three times and returned home with $60. The man realized that he can survive this way, and started to go every day earlier and return late. Thus, his money doubled or tripled every day. Shortly, he bought a cart, then a truck, and then he had his own fleet of delivery vehicles. 5 years later, the man is one of the biggest food retailers in the Harare.

He started to plan his family's future, and decided to have a life insurance. He called an insurance broker, and chose a protection plan. When the conversation was concluded, the broker asked him for his email. The man replied, "I don't have an email."

The broker answered curiously, "You don't have an email, and yet have succeeded to build an empire. Can you imagine what you could have been if you had an email?!!"

The man thought for a while and replied, "yes, I'd be an office boy at Microsoft!".

With your entrepreneurial mindset, there may be some businesses you cannot do. But certainly there are tens of others you can do successfully. The key to success is preparation and adequate planning.

CAREER CHANGE

From the foregoing, the basic problem facing an average employee today is that of career change. Moving from being an employee to being a self employed entrepreneur or business owner can be very threatening. This, most times has to do with the fear of losing your regular monthly pay. It becomes more threatening when you do not have enough savings or any savings at all. I advise people to save while still holding regular employment. You do this by cutting down on avoidable consumptions.

I must, however add that there is no amount of savings you

have that will be enough to remove the fear of losing your regular paycheck. There is no amount of savings that would be enough to save a new entrepreneur from the initial challenges of the business world. Entrepreneurship requires the highest level of responsibility and discipline. It takes a lot of planning and committed execution of plans.

I have been on the interview panels, where you have job applicants, whose previous organizations have either become distressed, moribund or rescued by government. It is like routine to see members of the interview panels asking the candidate about the causes of failure of the former organisation. Many such organizations are banks, manufacturing companies and other financial institutions. The interesting thing is that candidates seem to have a standard answer when asked about the causes of failure of the former company. They all blame the failure on the bad management at the top of the organisations. If the candidate was one of the people at the top management of his former employer; he normally blames the board members, shareholders or even the government policies for the failure of the previous employers. None of the several such candidates I have interviewed has ever acknowledged that he or she contributed in any way to the failure of the former organisation. It is easy to blame any other person for the failure of an organisation because you are an employee. For an entrepreneur, he takes full responsibility. Anybody can claim responsibility for success, but it takes high level of discipline to be ready to accept responsibility for failure.

MANAGING THE TRANSITION

The entrepreneur mindset is such that he is ready from the outset to accept responsibility for the outcomes of his decisions and actions. He is also aware that the outcomes may be positive or negative, success or failure. Hence, he does his best to reduce the chances of the outcomes being negative or failure.

Often times, when people attribute their inability to take bold steps out of paid job to own businesses to lack of capital or absence of enough savings, such people are not actually saying the truth. Most times the major problem is that those people are held bound by the fear of failure. They cannot just imagine what will happen to them if the outcome is a failure. They cannot imagine what other people will say or feel about them if their decisions turned out to be wrong. For meaningful success in any human endeavor, there is the need to conquer the fear of failure. It takes information, exposure and awareness to be able to do that. Adequate information and awareness will not only make successful outcomes of your decisions to become so real to you that you forget the possibility of failure. Information and awareness will also make you to know that failure is not a strange event. You will get to know that many of the world successful people are those who have previously tasted failure.

TYPES OF CAREER CHANGE
There is usually, two way movement from a paid employment. The first is when you have to move from one paid job to another paid job. Usually, you move from where

MANAGING THE TRANSITION

you are to a place with better offer. But many people have had to move to a job with worst condition than the previous one. This is either because you are not able to analyse the situation enough to be able to break down the new offer in both the intrinsic and extrinsic dimensions. At the end of the day, you have moved before you see the reality of the new employment. Sometimes, it is just because the employee is already desperate to change job that he has accepted an offer that is worst than the previous one in all ramifications. This is a problem which many people find difficult to manage.

Some people react to this problem by staying on a particular employment for a life time, 'till death do them part'. Others respond by moving from job to job in such a way that they never take enough time to learn the basic lessons of life in an employment which will be useful for their career. My goal is not to argue which of the two is better, being a moving employee or being a settler employee. We can leave this discussion for another day. It is enough to state that this is a problem that confronts every job holder. Where there is a problem, there is usually a solution. Seek advice, seek knowledge and get the necessary exposure to be able to overcome this common enemy. There are career counselors everywhere, you can talk to them.

The second type of movement from paid employment is moving from paid job to own business. I must state that managing transition from paid job to paid job and transition from paid job to own business requires relatively similar mindset and skills. They both require adequate planning and commitment to execution of plan. They both require adequate preparation, particularly in terms of information, awareness and life style. Self awareness, sincerity, discipline and expectation management are very essential in both scenarios. You must also have a very good sense of timing. The good thing is that all of these can be taught. They can be learnt. They can be cultivated and developed.

WHEN IT IS TIME FOR A CHANGE
I remember the story of one of my very good friends. We both worked in the same organisation years back. The company was a medium size organisation. Even though the company was doing very well in terms of profitability and expansion, the ownership revolved around a single family. This made the feeling of the chairman about you to mean almost everything within the organisation. While I was well favored by the chairman and even his family members, my friend was always less appreciated by the chairman. I personally felt my friend was trying his very best in terms of job delivery and even loyalty and commitment to the company. I also tried my best, unsuccessfully to bring him to the good book of the boss. At a point, I had to advise him to look for another job.

Within a very short period, he was able to secure a job that paid about 500% of his salary in our company. About a month after he moved to the new company, I gave him a very strange advice. I advised him not to settle down in the new employment until he has analysed the company and he is sure it is actually a place to stay and grow on long term basis. I could see the strange look on his face. What do you mean by that, he seemed to be asking me? That kind of analysis will not be necessary in this kind of company, I could hear him saying with his body language. Of course, the company was a multinational company. It was what is called a conglomerate in the business world. Because of our level of closeness, he simply thanked me and we closed the discussion. I was, however too sure he was not going to do anything about that kind of advice. Exactly six months in the company, almost all of them who joined the company at the same time were laid off.

My recommended analysis probably would have helped my friend to escape the sad occurrence. Such analysis is not only necessary when joining a company newly, you must, from time to time analyse the future of the organisation where you earn your living. You need to take your analysis beyond the company to the entire industry or the sector of the economy where your company operates. Companies die a long time before the public becomes aware of their demise. Many of these companies, even after they are fundamentally dead, still continue to hire new employees and engage in expansion projects. These may be in an attempt to rescue the company or in an attempt to deceive the public. Wisdom will help you to know when to move. I rejected an employment offer at the last minutes simply because of some information I got by asking my lawyer to conduct a legal search on the company. It cost me money to conduct the search, but it has saved me from possible major career disaster.

ORGANIZATIONAL SCANNING
The following may help you to know when to move, usually before a lot of other people are aware

1. How viable is your current organisation: As a trainer, I have had to ask my trainees critical questions about their organization. The experience is that more than 80% employees do not bother to know basic things concerning the present and future survival of their company. Majority of employees are those who only know about their monthly salaries and the latest gossip in the company. The most surprising thing, sometimes, is when you discovered that such an employee has been in that company for more than a decade. Yet, he does not know the key owners of the organisation, their business and family history. Some do not even know the mission, vision and core objectives of the company. You can be sure that such people will not even know much about profitability, potentials and going concern position of the company. Sometimes, the profitability the company shows on paper and to the public is not actually the true profitability.

There are companies doing practically no business, yet

declaring huge profit year in year out. These are just paper profits declared for the purpose of deceiving the public. Many companies, particularly financial institutions are in the habit of hiring financial officers who specialise in creative accounting or financial engineering just to be able to deceive the public. As a professional in the field for more than a decade, I know you can only hide your true position in the short run. In the long run, there cannot be any hideout for poor performance. We know people who have done this in the past and we can also tell where they are today. We also know people who are doing it right now and can tell where they will be in the nearest future. One way you know these companies is that, even their financial information that are legally supposed to be public document are protected even from there senior employees the way people protect salt from rain. The point is that even if the public does not know the true state of your organization, you as an employee of the company must know.

Not knowing basic information about the company you work for is like the case of a spouse making marriage commitment to a man or a woman he does not know anything about. Even where these are kept as top secret, you must make serious effort to know, in your own interest. Where it is impossible to get the basic information about your employer, you must be able to take decision on whether to exit or stay in such organisation depending on the relevance and seriousness of the information that is being kept secret. I must also add that, where you have vital information about your company, you must be able to keep it top secret while you use it for your personal decision and planning. If you cannot interpret the information available to you, ask hypothetical questions from people who are specialist in that area. If the information clearly shows the company is not viable or will not be viable in the nearest future, you need to quickly plan your exit. You must know that any information you got like this is for your own consumption. Since you are not the official spokesperson of the organisation, at no time will you divulge sensitive information to the public about your company.

2.   How solid and orderly is the management of the business: Viability of a company is largely determined by the ownership and management. However, most times the management plays prominent and critical roles that their activities are enough to predict the future of the company. Secondly, the attitudes and practices of the top management of a company are subtle reflection of the kind of ownership behind the company. Recklessness of the management may either be a reflection of reckless ownership or board. At other times, it may be a reflection of the fact that the board is weak, lacks knowledge or has abdicated it oversight functions.

The summary is that as an employee, you need to be sensitive as to what the management does or it does not do. Where you are not sure about anything, ask questions.

MANAGING THE TRANSITION

3. Have you been stagnated in the same position and pay for a long time? : I have heard people complain of being stagnated on the same grade or the same salary for five to ten years in an employment? This should be an issue of serious concern to both the employees and the employer. But our focus here is the employee. It is either the employee is not productive or the company is moving backwards. Even where the employee is not productive, no good and progressive employer will be comfortable keeping somebody stagnated for so long a time. It is either you do your best to ensure the employee improves or the employee is exited from your system. There is much negative contribution of the stagnated employee which we cannot possibly discuss in this book.

The bottom line is that long stagnation is a serious pointer that something is wrong. Your critical analysis of the situation will lead you as to whether you should change your job or your attitude.

4. Can you clearly see a career path on the job: Even in a profitable and growing organisation, you must be able to see that there are higher functions and positions you can aspire to within the company. Your growth within the organisation must also be as predictable as possible. There have been cases of chief executives ending their career in the most unceremonious way in recent years. Many of them, helmsmen of giant financial institutions and multinational corporations. These are often people who performed excellently when they got to such prestigious position. In my opinion, many of these chief executives have one thing in common. They are people who have over stayed in that position and have started psychologically to experience diminishing return. They are people who have no higher goals to aspire to, and therefore want to consolidate their achievement via a sit tight strategy. They become so afraid of vacating their exalted offices that they are ready to break any establish rules to ensure they stay on. They get busy ensuring their personal survival that the organisations continue to suffer and retrogress. Many of these corporate leaders have the same in common with political leaders who try to perpetuate themselves in office. There are religious leaders who also try to perpetuate themselves in office.

Psychologically, human beings are not designed to be stagnated. We are made to continue to aspire and press for the heights until we breathe our last. Even where you are running a personal or family business, you must continue to rebrand and restructure in such a way that there are new things to look forward to everyday. Of course, no matter how private or personal it may be, there must be a succession plan. Even as a young graduate, I got to know both by studying and by intuition, that staying too long on one function till you become too familiar is risky. Even within the same organization, I have always made it so clear that after three years on a function, I will be expecting a new role or I begin to plan my exit from that system. It has always worked for me. That I have always left excellent record in all the roles I have handled may not be unconnected with this wisdom.

Therefore, when you find yourself in such a situation, where there are no higher roles to aspire to and you are not in a position to create one, it may mean that there is a need to exit the system. Your exit may be to another employment or to your own business. The important thing is that you must know when the game is already getting over.

5.   Are you at the peak : Just like our discussion above, if you are at the peak of the organisation or the function, it is a natural pointer to the fact that you need to look for a higher or an alternative challenge for yourself.

6.   Are you handling additional responsibilities because the organisation is downsizing without additional pay or benefits: Often times, when one person is doing the job naturally meant for two or more persons, it is a pointer to the fact that sustainability of the organisation is in danger. Many so called restructuring are survival strategies adopted by drowning organisations. I do not mean that any organisation that is undergoing restructuring has a survival problem. Good and growing companies also restructure. In fact, the fact that an organisation does not restructure over a long period of time may be an indication that the company will not be able to survive in a changing environment. Yours is to do your analysis based on internal and external information to be able to predict the likely future outcomes.

7. **Are there higher level employees leaving - high turnover:** When you see more senior people exiting an organisation in quick succession, it is an indication that you need to watch and ask questions. Usually, these senior people have the information about the company which is not known to the junior employees and the general public. Sometimes, it is only one key senior person who left in a very controversial circumstance. It is either that the management cannot give explanation or it gives very flimsy explanation. You need to analyse the situation alongside your internal knowledge of the organisation to be able to decide on your line of action.

8. **Are there company bills pilling up so much:** When a company is finding it difficult to meet its financial obligations as and when due, it is often an indication that something may be wrong. The obligations may be to the employees or any other parties. Even where the company has the capability to pay but the management is becoming notorious for default obligation, it is a pointer that something is wrong or something may soon be wrong.

It must also be said that it is not all the time an organisation is facing a challenge that the right decision for you is to exit the organisation. There may be very good opportunity for you in an organisation that is passing through challenges or is restructuring, particularly when the management and the owners are taking the right steps to address the challenges and you are positive that the situation is not beyond redemption.

Your personal analysis will tell you the right direction to go. Where you are not sure, ask people who are more experienced.

9. Are you unclear about the company's direction, goals or mission: It is possible that the company you work for does not have a clearly articulated mission, vision, goals and corporate objectives. It is also possible that there are clear goals and mission which are known to only one person - the boss or a very few people. If you find yourself in this kind of environment, particularly where there is nothing you can do about it, you need to reevaluate your staying in that organisation. Even when the company is still making profit, it is a matter of time. A company without clear goals, mission, vision and corporate objectives is not going far. And where all these are available but are not properly communicated to the members of the organization, such a system is not better than a place where no one exists.

10. Are the company assets being sold or there is a buy-out or asset stripping: Whenever you see the major assets of the company been sold without replacement, it is an indication the company is parking up. There was a sad story of a man who was even the chief maintenance engineer responsible for the valuation of all the assets of the company that are being disposed at give away prices. He even bought one of the assets. Yet, he was not aware his days were numbered in that employment. It was the day he got his letter of termination of employment he knew the game was over.

A very sensitive analysis of the situation would have saved him the pain. He could have planned to exit to his own business, particularly as there were company assets he could buy legitimately at give away prices. He could have also planned an exit to another paid job.

PERSONAL SCANNING

We can now zero down to people who are exiting paid job to own business. We can also apply this to people who want to move without any paid job straight to their own business. The most critical issue here is personal preparation. You must be prepared and be sure you are prepared. Most times, the only preparation people know about is that of startup capital. There is more to the business life than capital. Knowledge is actually the most critical thing. Adequate knowledge will tell you how to raise the money you need. Emotional preparation is equally more important than financial preparation. Without adequate knowledge of what you want to do and strong emotional stability in relation to money and people management, you stand to lose any amount of money you carry into starting a business.

There is the need for personal examination and self assessment. There are critical questions you need to ask yourself. I have divided the questions into two categories. The first, I call the **personal conversation questions**. These have to do with those things that go on within you and their implication to your success in a startup business. The second category, I call **personal contribution questions**. They have to do with your contribution to wherever you currently find yourself. Success in any life endeavor is not a destination but a journey. And that journey is a lifelong one. Everyday you live is part of the journey. If you are an employee who does not give his best on the job, never think you will give your best when you get into your own business. It means you can actually predict your future by assessing your level of preparation based on what you currently do and your contribution to your current organisation. The good news is that, anybody can change. There is always room for personal development and cultivation.

To the personal conversation questions, you will be advised to provide a sincere 'yes' or 'no' response. You can then measure yourself based on the overall score. On each of the personal contribution question, you will be required to grade yourself on a scale of 1 to 5. Again, being sincere to yourself is the key. You will also need to measure your preparedness for your own business based on your overall score out of a total of 100.

The essence of the personal conversation is for you to determine whether you actually need a change of what you do. That change may be to another paid job or to own business. Personal contributions questions will help you to assess whether you are prepared for your own business. Where you are not prepared, you can start the preparation even today.

PERSONAL CONVERSATION QUESTIONS
1. My career ambition cannot be fulfilled at my present company and I wouldn't mind resigning, even if I have to stay without job for the next 3-4 months. Yes/No
2. My job no longer fits my personal goals, suits my skills or matches my basic interest. I wouldn't mind a change even with a lower income temporarily. Yes/No
3. I feel stressed or depressed on days off when I think about going back to work and I am certain nothing can be done on my part to improve this situation Yes/No
4. I have said to myself repeatedly, this pay isn't worth it. I have discovered something else that motivates me and I am ready to give it a trial. Yes/No.
5. Aside my present job, I have tried something else and I am positive it will give me higher yield and fulfillment compared to what I do at present. Yes/No.
6. I am a master planner, a strategist and I have demonstrated this by contributing immensely to the growth of my past and present organisations. Yes/No

PERSONAL CONTRIBUTION QUESTIONS
1. During problem solving discussions with co-workers, are you usually the one to come up with the solutions that eventually get enacted?
   1   2   3   4   5
2. Do you respond to most of your day-to-day problems with the financial health of the company as a major consideration?

MANAGING THE TRANSITION

      1   2   3   4   5

3. Are you frustrated when you see evidence of wasteful spending and an attitude that says, "it is not my money, I seriously do not care"?
      1   2   3   4   5

4. Have you become known as the person who gets the assignments that are too difficult for others to accomplish?
      1   2   3   4   5

5. When you fail at a task, do you take it as a challenge, resulting in an increased desire to figure out how to succeed?
      1   2   3   4   5

6. Are you comfortable making multiple attempts before eventually solving difficult challenges?
      1   2   3   4   5

7. Have some of the most significant raises, bonuses and promotions come from showing your stuff first, without agreeing to incentive in advance?
      1   2   3   4   5

8. Are you confident that when your superiors see the outcomes you produce, they will try to adequately recognize and reward you, as they are able?
      1   2   3   4   5

9. Do you believe that even if your excellent work is not immediately rewarded, you will ultimately benefit because of your knowledge and experience?
      1   2   3   4   5

10. Are you the last person your co-workers would come to

when 'venting' about how unfairly they were treated by so-and-so in a recent meeting or within the organization?
1   2   3   4   5

11. Do you hold others accountable when they engage in self-promoting behaviors at the expense of the company?
1   2   3   4   5

12. Have you had a track record of success when attempting to steer personal conversations and time-wasting distractions back to the core business?
1   2   3   4   5

13. Are you regularly given written materials to proofread one last time before they go out?
1   2   3   4   5

14. Do your teammates most often choose you to make crucial presentation to management, clients or prospects?
1   2   3   4   5

15. Are you called upon frequently to explain processes and procedures to new hires, or to deal with highly irritated customers?
1   2   3   4   5

16. What is your present skill level on the following?
a. Business finance
1   2   3   4   5
b. Sales & Marketing
1   2   3   4   5
c. People management
1   2   3   4   5
d. Problem solving

MANAGING THE TRANSITION

       1   2   3   4   5
e.   Communication
       1   2   3   4   5

Scoring
If you scored
0 – 60 = you should keep your day job or move to another paid job
61-90 = you have potential and can improve with effort to become a business owner. Read books and get relevant coaching in the categories where you are weak. When you start your business, hire for strength in any area where you remain less satisfactory.
91-100 = print your business cards, set up your website and finish your business plan. You can roll out your business even today.

FROM PAID JOB TO OWN BUSINESS
On a final note, I must give some pieces of advice to those who are moving from paid job to own business. I can tell you that is the way to go. The labour market all over the world is saturated. The world of entrepreneurship is the answer.

1. The best time to start your business is when you are still young and strong: it is the height of self deceit to assume you will start your own business when you retired from paid employment. The general explanation people give for waiting even on a paid job that does not promise them a future is that they want to wait till they are able to save enough money. The reality around us is that people hardly save enough money until retirement. That is why our professors in the universities were fighting that their retirement age be made 70years instead of 65years.

You need energy to successfully run a startup business. If you want to own your own business, start when you still have the energy. The business you start at retirement can only be a pastime.

2. First get the knowledge for your desired business: use the time you are on a paid job to seek knowledge of the business you intend to go into. It is advisable you seek the general knowledge about a number of businesses. From them, you can select the one you know is best for you. Then learn the details of your selected option. It is not always possible for you to learn enough of your new business while still keeping another paid job. There are some business lessons you can only learn by practice. All you need is to learn as much as possible.

Then selectively associate yourself with people who are already successfully doing what you want to start doing. Keep in touch with them, both before and after you must have started you own. The bottom line is that you must acknowledge the fact that knowledge and skill are much more important than money. The money you have without knowledge is the money you will soon lose.

MANAGING THE TRANSITION

3. Seek first knowledge and money will follow: money naturally follows after problem solving knowledge and skills. Part of the critical knowledge of a particular type of business is the knowledge of what money you need and how to raise money for that type of business. Every business has a peculiar way of raising money for it. There is a particular way of raising money for a real estate business. There is a particular way to raise money for agricultural business.

4. Test the Waters: do some experiments before you go full force.

5. Use Other People's Experience to Learn - Don't Reinvent the Wheel: you don't need to do an entirely new thing. You can take a lot from what others have successfully done. Then add your own innovation.

6. Take the plunge and jump off the comfort of your salary. Paycheck has a way of holding people back. Avoid this temptation. Take the risk. Not taking risk is actually riskier.

THE BEST WAY TO START

11

CHOOSING THE RIGHT BUSINESS FOR YOURSELF

A major mistake to avoid in starting a business is that of choosing the wrong business. Wrong choice accounts for 80% of business and life failures. It is also important that you choose the business for yourself, not another person choosing it for you. People can advise you, they can guide you or even provide the needed financial support for the business. But never allow them decide for you.

Choosing it yourself is the first step in the right direction. If you choose by yourself you would be ready to take responsibility for its success or failure; and that alone will

THE BEST WAY TO START

help you to go all the way, giving it all it takes.

The process of choosing is the most essential and the most tasking. That process would afford you the opportunity to gather the preliminary information and get the primary knowledge.

There are two problems here. The two are natural and common to all men. However, the day you solve the two problems in your life, that day you have taken the first step on the ladder of greatness and fulfillment.

FEAR OF FAILURE
Nobody wants to identify with failure. But avoiding failure also may mean avoiding success. Instead of avoiding failure, look for the right knowledge and skills that guarantee success in your choice area of business. The time you take in doing that is never a waste; you will reap it in hundred folds later.

AVOIDING RESPONSIBILITY
Because people are not ready to identify with failure, they usually look for whom to blame for their failure. Be ready to take responsibility for your actions and decisions, whether they turn out good or bad. The joy of it is that when you are ready to take responsibility, most of your actions and decisions will always turn out good. Why? Because you will always give it the care and commitment it deserves.

The under-listed factors are essential if you want to choose the right business. Remember, the right business for me may not always be the right one for you. The fact that it brings money for the people that are in it is not enough proof that it is right or good for you.

FIND YOUR PASSION
The right business for you is the one that goes along with your passion. What are your hobbies and interests? They must relate to the business you are doing. I am sure you will not say my passion is getting rich or making money. That is just an end result, a consequence of applying your passion rightly.

Your passion is something you enjoy doing, even without expecting money. Teaching and motivating people to a better living and achievement are what I am passionate about. Helping others solve their problems has always been part of me. I have done that for years without monetary rewards or promise. I enjoy spreading any good idea I am aware of for the benefit of others. That is my life style. Your passion is your life style and to be successful, you need to choose business that relates to your passion.

CAPITALISE ON YOUR STRENGTH
All of us are gifted and talented. Your major assignment is to identify your gifts and talents and profit with them. You can ask other people who know you closely. You will be surprised they know certain things about you that you don't even know about yourself.

Your experience, training and education are all parts of your strengths. See how they can be used in line with your passion to bring out a money making idea. I remember I asked one of my mentors, why he chose the business he is doing that has made him very successful. He simply answered me; **"because that is what I knew how to do"**. Know your strengths and capitalize on them.

ASSESS MARKETABILITY
Passion and talents are great, but they can only give you money by applying them to produce something people are ready to pay for. That is what marketability is all about. Business success comes by meeting customer's needs or demand. Creating value is the key. What do people buy?

Benefit, Satisfaction and solution to their problems. Customers exchange money for something they believe will give them benefit or satisfaction above the value of money they pay for it.

How do you determine marketability from the beginning? Ask people, find out their needs. Look and study people who have been in the same or similar business. Study the economic trend in your locality or country. Think about what fashion is in vogue. Read about the business you want to start, ask questions about it. Negative response from people does not naturally mean your idea will not sell. It may simply mean you have not packaged it in the form that people will appreciate. The type of people you choose to ask question is also very important. Some people are generally negative; they don't like new ideas and innovations. Avoid those people. Look for people who are very objective and positively analytical.

Just that people who are already in the same or similar business are complaining does not mean there is no opportunity for good profit in that area of business again. It may only mean they have not discovered the best way to doing it.

START SMALL
Always start out small, avoiding big cash outlay at the beginning. Take one step at a time but make sure you start, don't procrastinate. It is advisable that you start with money you can afford to lose, especially when you have a current source of income, no matter how small. In fact, that is about the only advantage of taking up a paid job. Whatever risk you take while still holding your current employment, your salary is the security. If you lose this month salary, you are still expecting next month pay. That is always a good point to start and experiment as much and as long as you wish. But never plan your future on salary; it will always disappoint.

Start slowly and gradually build your business. For example, don't buy new office equipment when you can make do with some used ones. Allow the already buoyant people to buy new latest car, then you can buy it from them after one year for less than half market price. Go step by step, constantly testing the market. Stay with the product lines that work and eliminate those that are duds. With these principles, you will surely grow; it is just a matter of time. Avoid get rich quick ideas. Verify ideas very well before you invest in them. However, don't ignore any new idea. No idea is too good to be real.

START WHERE YOU ARE
It is often to hear people saying they want to travel somewhere to start business. There is nothing wrong in changing location for business reasons. Because, location is one of the factors that determine business success. But that is not applicable to people who have not exploited the opportunities in their current location. It is cheaper to start business in a place you are well familiar with. It is easier to adjust in a place you know so well when things go wrong. Don't quit your job to start a business when you can easily combine the two.

START WITH WHAT YOU HAVE
A good business for you is the one that requires what you have or what you can get with reasonable cost and within a reasonable time. Anyone that demands what you never had nor can get is not meant for you, no matter what it promises. Business will normally demand something from you. The good news is that there is nobody that has nothing to give for business purpose. If you don't have money you have time, you have your brain and some of us have certificates that are

worth more than money, if we know how to use them. Your experience and connection are all very useful in business. While money is always in short supply, all these other factors are there in abundance. Put them to use, they will give you all the money you need.

START WITH WHAT YOU KNOW
Never go into a business you don't understand. If you have desire or interest in something you know little or nothing about, start by gathering the right knowledge.

START NOW
Avoid procrastination. The reason why you need to start small where you are, with what you have and with what you know is for you to start now without any excuse for procrastination. Early to bed is early to rise. The time is now.

START ANYHOW
It is better you try and fail than to fail to try. If you are a perfectionist, you will like to avoid anything called mistake. But great people in the world are not the people who avoid mistakes; they are those who learn from mistakes.

If you are a perfectionist, there is no problem about that. Only learn to know when to apply your perfectionist ideology. It is not applicable all the time. Trying to be a perfectionist all the time is a demonstration of pride and an attempt to please people all the time.